E. F. BENSON

Mr Benson remembered in Rye, and the world of Tilling

Cynthia and Tony Reavell

PREFACE BY SIR STEVEN RUNCIMAN

Martello Bookshop

1 Cover: Designed by Michael Renton, artwork by Adams of Rye.
Studio portrait of E. F. Benson by Claude Harris.

Printed in Great Britain by Headley Brothers Ltd, The Invicta Press, Ashford, Kent, and London

For Aubrey Woods who introduced us and so many others to the delights of the Mapp & Lucia novels through his incomparable radio readings of them.

Contents

Illustrations

Acknowledgments, and Books by E. F. Benson 1

Preface 7

Introduction 9

Part I E. F. Benson and Lamb House

1 E. F. Benson—his family background and the years before Rye 11

2 Lamb House—a short history, before the Bensons lived there 16

3 E. F. Benson—an outline of his Rye years 19

4 E. F. Benson's private life 24

5 Benson windows in St Mary's Parish Church, Rye 27

Part II Charlie Tomlin's memories

1 Charlie's early years 31

2 Life in Rye and London 41

3 Mr Benson's friends and his death 47

Part III Memories of Mr Benson by others

1 Ivy Robbins 57

2 Constance Warrender, and others 59

3 Sir Steven Runciman, and others 67

Part IV Tilling and fellow inhabitants of Benson's Rye—with introduction

1 Order of events in the Tilling novels 75

2 Tilling topography 79

3 Tilling residents 84

4 Some origins for Tilling characters and situations 87

5 Fellow inhabitants of Benson's Rye 91

Index 99

Illustrations

1 E. F. Benson, studio portrait (Front Cover)
2 Tremans, Horsted Keynes
3 Lamb House and Garden Room
4 E. F. Benson, 1920's
5 Lamb House garden party
6 Charlie Tomlin as a young man
7 Gabriel the gardener
8 Charlie Tomlin with Taffy
9 Charlie Tomlin in the 1960's or 1970's
10 Tatler photograph of E. F. Benson and friends on a skating holiday
11 Lamb House staff, 1939
12 E. F. Benson with friends
13 Rye group, 1938 or 1939
14 Map of Tilling, by Katharine Stephen (page 74)
15 Garden Room interior
16 F. Yeats-Brown and E. F. Benson
17 E. F. Benson in the Secret Garden
18 E. F. Benson, early 1930's
19 E. F. Benson, studio portrait
20 E. F. Benson receives the Freedom of the Borough from Rye Borough Council 1938
21 Cartoon by Philip Burne-Jones

Illustration credits: Martello Bookshop, 1, 2, 3, 4, 5, 6, 7, 8, 12, 14, 18, 19, 20; J. Wood, 9; Tatler, 10; Mrs Robbins, 11, 16, 17; Mrs Warrender, 13; the Executors of the Estate of K. S. P. McDowall, 15, 21.

Acknowledgments

We would like to thank the following people for all their assistance, and we would particularly like to say how kind and helpful we found everyone (with a single exception!) in their willingness to give up time to talk and write to us. We very much appreciate their co-operation and interest:

Dr John Aiken; Mrs Elizabeth Ashby; Betty Askwith; Geoffrey Bagley; Mrs Viola Bayley; Mrs Gwen Bligh; William Bryan; William Carey; Mrs Clara Carnell; Miss Cotton; Mrs Betty Crosskill; Mr Kenneth Ellis; Mrs Mildred Ellis; Mrs Patricia Fallace; Percy Fletcher; Mrs John Hacking; Mrs Eric Mason; Mrs Myfanwy Mickleson; John Munday of the National Maritime Museum; Major Boris Mylne; Mrs Kathleen Mylne; Frederick Orford; Mr Palmer; David Parker; Mr Parsons; Miss S. B. S. Pigrome; Miss Veronica Powles; Geoffrey Prentice; David Reavell; Tamsyn Reavell; Lady Ritchie; Mrs Ivy Robbins; The Hon. Sir Steven Runciman; Mrs Alice Russell; George Rylands; Mrs Marian Shephard; John Smith; Miss Josepha Aubrey Smith; Mr and Mrs Sam Standen; Katharine Stephen; Arthur and Margaret Tiltman; Miss Edith Turner; Mrs Van den Bosch; Dr Alec Vidler; Mrs Constance Warrender; A. P. Watt Ltd, Literary agents (and in particular Linda Shaughnessy); Mrs Margaret Wethey; J. Wood; John Wyse.

We would also like to thank the following for permission to quote from books and newspaper articles:

Bodley Head: *Day in, Day out* by Mrs Aubrey le Blond (1928, o.p.); Chatto & Windus: *As We Were* (1930), *As We Are* (1932) and *Final Edition* (1940) by E. F. Benson, and *Two Victorian Families* by Betty Askwith (1971, o.p.); the Executors of the Estate of K. S. P. McDowall for E. F. Benson's three volumes of autobiography named above (Hogarth reprints announced for 1985), and also *Our Family Affairs* (Cassell 1920, o.p.) and *Travail of Gold* (1933, o.p.); Brian Masters and Hamish Hamilton for their *Now Barabbas was a Rotter* (1978, o.p.); Martello Bookshop for *Rye Colour Guide* (1982) and the Tilling map (1984) and some of the photographs; the *Sussex Express* and its editor Peter Austin for reports and obituary.

And special thanks to Heinemann for allowing us to draw so heavily on the *Mapp & Lucia* novels, and for having the vision to keep them in print for all these years—all the hardbacks have been in print since 1970: *Queen Lucia* (1920); *Miss Mapp* (1922); *Lucia in London* (1927); *The Male Impersonator* (1928); *Mapp & Lucia* (1931—incidentally, Benson originally intended calling this *The Queens of Tilling*); *Lucia's Progress* (1935); *Trouble for Lucia* (1939). Corgi's Black Swan has also paper-backed all the novels in 1984, with splendid new covers by Lynda Riess.

Note: o.p. means out-of-print, with no known plans to reprint.

Other books consulted

Deacon's Rye Directories 1920–40; G. P. Jacomb-Hood's *With brush and with pencil* (1925, o.p.); H. Montgomery Hyde's *The Story of Lamb House* (1975, publ. by the National Trust and inexplicably o.p.); David Newsome's *Godliness and Good Learning* (John Murray, 1961); David Newsome's *On the Edge of Paradise* (John Murray, 1980); Richard Ormrod's *Una Troubridge* (Jonathan Cape, 1984); *The Parish Church of St Mary the Virgin, Rye* (Pitkin); David Williams's *Genesis and Exodus* (Hamish Hamilton, 1979, o.p.); Rye, Winchelsea and District Memorial Hospital's *A Cargo of Recipes* (1936, o.p.).

Books by E. F. Benson
(nf) means non-fiction
(s) means short stories

1888 Sketches from Marlborough (anon.)
1893 Dodo
Six Common Things (s)
1894 The Rubicon
A Double Overture (s)
1895 The Judgment Books
1896 Limitations
1897 The Babe, B.A.
1898 The Money Market
The Vintage
1899 The Capsina
Mammon and Company
1900 The Princess Sophia
1901 The Luck of the Vails
1902 Scarlet and Hyssop
1903 An Act in a Backwater
The Relentless City

The Valkyres
The Book of Months
1904 The Challoners
1905 The Image in the Sand
Diversions Day by Day (nf) (E. F. B. and Eustace Miles)
They also wrote: Daily Training (nf) at about this time
1906 The Angel of Pain
The House of Defence
Paul
1907 Sheaves
1908 The Climber
The Blotting Book
English Figure Skating (nf)
1909 A Reaping
1910 Daisy's Aunt
(The Fascinating Mrs Halton—U.S. edition of Daisy's Aunt)
The Osbornes
1911 Juggernaut
(Margery—U.S. edition of Juggernaut)
Account Rendered
1912 Mrs Ames
The Room in the Tower (s)
Bensoniana (E. F. B. quotes)
1913 Dodo's Daughter
Thorley Weir
The Weaker Vessel
Winter Sports in Switzerland (nf)
1914 Arundel
1915 The Oakleyites
1916 Mike/Michael
David Blaize
The Freaks of Mayfair
1917 An Autumn Sowing
Mr Teddy
(The Tortoise—U.S. edition of Mr Teddy)
1918 David Blaize and the Blue Door
Up and Down
The White Eagle of Poland (nf)
Mother (nf)

	Crescent and Iron Cross (nf)
1919	Across the Stream
	Robin Linnet
1920	Queen Lucia
	The Countess of Lowndes Square (s)
	Our Family Affairs (nf)
1921	Dodo Wonders
	Lovers and Friends
1922	Miss Mapp
	Peter
1923	Colin
	Visible and Invisible (s)
1924	Alan
	David of King's
1925	Colin II
	Rex
1926	Mezzanine
	Pharisees and Publicans
1927	Lucia in London
	Sir Francis Drake (nf)
1928	Spook Stories
	The Male Impersonator (s)
	Life of Alcibiades (nf)
1929	Paying Guests
	Ferdinand Magellan (nf)
1930	The Inheritor
	The Step (s)
	As We Were (nf)
1931	Mapp and Lucia
1932	Secret Lives
	As We Are (nf/f)
	Charlotte Bronte (nf)
1933	Travail of Gold
	King Edward VII (nf)
	The Outbreak of War (nf)
1934	Ravens' Brood
	More Spook Stories (s)
1935	Lucia's Progress
	Queen Victoria (nf)

1936 The Kaiser and English Relations (nf)
1937 Old London (four vols.)
1938 Queen Victoria's Daughters (nf)
1939 Trouble for Lucia
1940 Final Edition (nf)

Total: 97 books. 77 are fiction (including 8 of short stories) and 20 are non-fiction (including 2 jointly written books).

After compiling this list we were told of three further titles, dates and classifications not known: 1. The Book of Golf; 2. The Cricket of Abel; 3. Hirst and Shrewsbury. Two plays, Aunt Jeannie and Dinner at Eight, may also have been published.

Preface

For the elderly there are few experiences more irritating than of reading books about men and women whom they knew, written by authors of a generation to whom their victims were unknown. These biographers are often scrupulous in their study of the sources, but they are insensitive to the atmosphere of the past and unaware of that transient element, its humour, taking with deadly seriousness and adding trendy psychoanalytical explanations to words and deeds that were light-hearted in origin. It is therefore a great pleasure to introduce a work that is based on the memories of friends of E. F. Benson who really knew him. We must be particularly grateful for the inclusion of the memories of Charlie Tomlin, his devoted manservant, who knew him better than anyone and on whom he depended wholly for his welfare.

It is to be doubted if E. F. Benson's earlier books will ever come back into fashion, though his volumes of memories are well worth reading. But the renascent popularity of his Tilling novels is a tribute to the timelessness of his wit and his kindly enjoyment of human vanity and folly.

Steven Runciman

Introduction

When in 1978 we met Charlie Tomlin, Mr Benson's manservant from 1918 to his death in 1940, and he talked so vividly about his master, we realised that these memories must be captured before it was too late. Conversation with him led us to talk to other people in Rye who remembered Mr Benson, in however slight or apparently trivial a connection, and to build up a picture of Rye in the twenties and thirties, the Tilling of Mr Benson's *Mapp and Lucia* novels. Charlie's sudden death in 1981 showed the imperative need to record these memories as soon as possible.

In 1983 we took over from Miss Fay Hodges the Tilling Society, a light-hearted grouping of Benson enthusiasts. Receiving and providing information for the Society led us to explore further the correspondence between the fictional Tilling and the real Rye of that period, both in its topography and its personalities. This relationship intrigues so many people that it seemed helpful to publish the result of our researches together with the Rye memories of Mr Benson. We have also included the acute and sympathetic recollections of Sir Steven Runciman who has been so very generous of his time.

Most of our material is taken from people talking about the past of forty to sixty years ago, and, memory being such a fallible instrument, there are bound to be at least some errors of fact and areas of disagreement in spite of our careful checking. But we hope that people will come forward to correct and expand where they have knowledge, so that the record can be amended. One difficulty is the spelling of names of places and people, particularly in the case of Charlie Tomlin who spoke softly and to whom we could no longer refer when checking his recorded voice.

No definitive picture emerges of the kind of man Mr Benson was in his Rye years. To his servants he was a good employer, someone they liked and trusted: to some neighbouring children a kind old gentleman, to others he appeared an austere and forbidding figure. On the whole it seems that he was reserved with those he did not know, perhaps even brusque in manner. He was of course in constant pain from arthritis. But to those he did know he was exceptionally good company, with a fund of humorous stories which displayed his brilliant wit and lively interest in humanity in all its aspects and actions. The victim in his books is pretence, it was hypocrisy he rode out to slay, and no doubt his conversation reflected this crusade. He had the sanity and self-knowledge to be able to laugh at himself as he does in his autobiographical writings.

His tastes were romantic—music, mountains, Hellenism, sun and sea, snow and forest—though most of these, like his athletic interests, were more evident in his youth than by the time he came to Rye. That he was much revered in Rye is shown by the offer to him of the mayoralty. In David Williams's 1979 biography of the Benson family (and his phrases and tone are repeated in 1980's reviews), he is astonishingly portrayed as a "malicious" "bitchy" misanthrope, specialising in "black humour" and even "celebrated for his homosexuality". If he had displayed these striking qualities at council meetings, it is odd that his colleagues re-elected him twice—or indeed that he was asked anywhere! The records make it clear that he in fact conducted these meetings with charm and courtesy. This was no humanity-hating old recluse ostracised in his castle, but a respected figure in the town with an extensive social life, particularly in London, which he enjoyed very much and in which he gave enjoyment to his friends as well.

The person who was closest to him all this time was Charlie Tomlin, and Charlie could say no ill of him. It is very easy when studying someone so closely as we have been doing to exaggerate their good qualities and ignore their weaknesses: but we can safely say of Mr Benson that he was a good employer, a man of ability and intelligence with an exceptional talent for discovering the absurd and pretentious, a man whose company was greatly relished by his friends, who did much for Rye both in his services and material gifts, and whose incomparable humour has enriched the lives of so many through his writings.

Part I

E. F. Benson and Lamb House

1 E. F. Benson—his family background and the years before Rye

(Most of the information for this section is taken from *Our Family Affairs*, publ. by Cassell in 1920.)

Edward Frederic Benson (Fred) was the most normal and straightforward member of a brilliant but eccentric and highly-charged family—"rather a close little corporation", as one brother, Arthur, was to describe it, ". . . we were rather unduly afraid of life." Their father, Edward White Benson, was possessed of a cold and single-minded Godliness, which he had developed even as a boy. At the age of eleven he built himself an oratory in an empty room; when his own father died when he was fourteen and his mother wanted to carry out his business plans and manufacture cobalt, Edward White Benson took what must even in those early Victorian days have seemed a priggish and high-handed stand. He virtually instructed her to give up all thought of running a business because it would seriously threaten his own career and his future in the church, and would damage his sisters' prospects. When seven years later his mother died penniless, leaving six children, he took it upon himself as head of the family to turn down an uncle's kind offer to adopt the youngest, on no other grounds than that this uncle was a Unitarian. Again, it is solely his own spiritual position which seems to have concerned him in his exceedingly unpleasant letters of rejection. When he was twenty-four, he took his twelve-year-old cousin, Mary Sidgwick, on his knee and asked her if she thought she would marry him when she grew up. This effectively blighted the rest of her childhood, and, still childishly innocent but wanting to please him and her mother, she married him when she was eighteen. She was an intelligent and demonstrative woman and the early years of marriage were hard for her, trying to live up to the expectations of her pious and censorious husband, while six children were born at fairly close intervals. Edward White Benson, whose good points included a powerful intellect and enormous energy, became the first headmaster of Wellington College in 1859.

Edward Frederic Benson was born at Wellington College on July

24th, 1867. The family nurse, Beth Cooper, was the person he was closest to for some years. (She had come from the household of Mary Benson's parents originally and she was to live on until 1911, when she was in her 90's and still with the family.) Then his mother emerged as a personality in his life but his father was just a rather remote and awe-inspiring presence at first. When Fred was six, his father was made Chancellor of the Diocese of Lincoln, and they moved there. The children were given a room which they called their museum, and so began their passion for collecting, with sheep's wool, pebbles, a dead hornet, butterflies, oxydised glass dug from the garden, broken clay pipes and fossils. Their mother taught them, and later they had governnesses, one of whom, a Miss Bramston, impressed them by being a Real Authoress. After that Fred went to a day school kept by a Mrs Giles. At this stage he came to dread his father for the disproportionate severity of his displeasure which, as three of the brothers wrote later, was too great for such trivial faults as unpunctuality, fidgetting or happy exuberance. This anger was quite unpredictable and the children, not knowing what would cause an outburst, learned to act "the prig and the hypocrite" in his presence, and were sad later at the thought that they were always so unnatural and constrained with him, when he really loved them deeply but was unable to show it, other than in strictness. He was also subject to black depressions.

Fred was excited at the discovery of the village of Riseholme (2½ miles from Lincoln) where the Bishop lived. The children always seemed to be allowed to do what they wanted here, and there were lakes and islands for fishing and boating, and they explored pathless places and ground up chestnuts with lake water, and pressed stinking waterweed and got "an awful fricassée of weed and paper". Fred and his sister, Maggie, became close friends and made up stories in which they and their collie, Watch, figured.

In 1877 Edward White Benson was made the first Bishop of Truro and they moved to a house called *Lis Escop* in the nearby village of Kenwyn where they had a glorious garden and grounds. They continued with their collecting, now adding birds' eggs (strictly regulated) and wild flowers, and Fred says that it was the names of these which gave him the beginnings of his love of words—centaury, comfrey, meadowsweet, bee-orchis, etc. The following year the oldest brother, his father's favourite, Martin, died; Fred had hardly known him, being so much younger, but his father was profoundly affected.

In 1878, Fred went to a private school at Temple Grove, East Sheen, for three years. Both teachers and head were distinctly eccentric and the life of the boys, as described in *David Blaize,* was "alternately uproarious and terror-stricken". He devoted himself to "games, stag-beetles and friendship". In the holidays the Benson children began their *Saturday Magazine,* already showing signs of their future prolific outputs. And their favourite game, which they invented, was the wild and energetic 'Pirates' which Fred later used in one of his short stories. The Bishop devoted his energies to organising the building of a cathedral at Truro; at this stage none of the rest of the family shared his ecclesiastical mind, not even Hugh (R.H.) who later became a Jesuit priest and came under the influence of the evil Baron Corvo (Frederick Rolfe) for a time. In his second year at this school, Fred's love of Bach, which stayed with him throughout his life, began with his piano lessons, and he found that the head's beautiful readings of beautiful English struck a chord. But, by the time he left this school, he was the scholastic failure of the family. He now became close to his younger brother, Hugh, with a secret language, and frequent quarrels and reconciliations. In the last holidays before changing schools in 1881 he went with the family to Switzerland, for the first time, and he first fell under the spell of the snow-covered mountains which were to mean so much to him.

At Marlborough School Fred spent some of his happiest years. His interest in games and sport developed, he won a competition for a butterfly collection he made in Savernake Forest (where he first came to love trees and solitary places) and he became involved in intense platonic friendships. He was strongly influenced by a gifted master, A. H. Beesly, who gave him the beginnings of his passionate interest in Greek and Latin, and all things Greek, and also introduced him to the game of rackets. In his second year, his father was made Archbishop of Canterbury, and so they moved to Lambeth, and Addington in the autumn and winter, with Augusts usually in Switzerland. Mary Benson was happiest at this period; her warm interest in people meant she thoroughly enjoyed entertaining, and Gladstone called her the "cleverest woman in Europe". The family went riding, did some shooting, played mini-golf and football, tobogganed, and skated on dreadful skates called Acmes or Caledonians, which clipped on to the boots, and often fell off. In the evenings they resumed their intellectual labours—music, painting, the *Saturday Magazine,* writing and acting plays (such as *The Spiritualist,* with a "slashing exposure of mediums"), argument and discussion, and voracious reading. Fred and Maggie began what finally emerged years later as *Dodo.* He writes also of the crushing boredom of Sundays, which had to be entirely devotional and without any sort of secular relaxation. This was a real pleasure, a festival, to the Archbishop—even if he did sometimes doze during readings from pious works—and he was unable to see how others felt about it. Even Prince Albert asked him if "there may not be too much excessive employment in Religious Exercise in the present system of [Wellington] College", but to no avail. Fred was made head of his house and captain of the school's Rugby Fifteen and then stayed on an extra year in which his great friend, Eustace Miles, was head boy. They became inseparable and concentrated exclusively on classics in order to get classical scholarships together at King's College, Cambridge, which they did in 1885. They also edited and wrote most of *The Marlburian.*

At Cambridge Eustace continued to be a good example in his capacity for long hours of study, broken by their strange games of indoor mini-tennis, and they eventually both got firsts in classics, although Fred stayed on and took an archaeology tripos. Monty James (M. R. James), who was a great mimic, was head of Fred's group and they were members of the Pitt Club and a literary society called the *Chitchat.* Professor Middleton fed his growing love of all things Greek by his infectious enthusiasm and, outside Cambridge, Fred fell completely under the spell of the American actress, Mary Anderson, and kept a photo of her by his bedside, although they didn't meet for another thirty years. His *Sketches from Marlborough* was published, and he began re-working *Dodo.* Nellie, another sister, died suddenly of diphtheria and Lucy Tait, daughter of the previous Archbishop of Canterbury, made her home with the Bensons. Mary Benson had always had deep emotional friendships with women, and this one lasted long after her husband's death, and indeed became almost a second and less demanding marriage.

When he left Cambridge, Fred got a grant to excavate at Chester, which he did so successfully that Gladstone sent for him. He sent *Dodo* to Henry James (who wrote kindly that the style wasn't as "ferociously literary" as he would like) and then left it awhile. It was finally published in 1893 when it "introduced a certain novelty into novel-writing which had quite a little vogue for a time". From 1892–5 he worked as an archaeologist in Greece and Egypt, at last seeing Athens where he had some comic encounters with the Greek royal family. And he met the enthusiastic and charming diplomat, Regie Lister, who became a good friend. Then in 1896 Archbishop Benson died in church at Hawarden, at Gladstone's side. The family spent that winter in Egypt, but were beset by illness. They returned and moved to Winchester, but soon Maggie, who had her own close friend, Nettie Gourlay, began to be jealous of her mother's friendship with Lucy Tait, feeling her own position as daughter was threatened. She also got obsessed with her father's memory, working on his papers and helping her older brother Arthur (A.C.) with a biography, gradually undergoing a personality change which often took the form of deep depressions, until she became insane; it culminated in 1906 in an unsuccessful homicidal attack, probably on her mother, although the object of the attack is nowhere specified in the family biographies. She was locked up in an asylum for the last ten years of her life, dying in 1916. She had been gifted and intelligent, getting a First in Moral Philosophy at Oxford, and then showing great talent both in organising archaeological excavations and in writing well-reasoned books.

In 1898 Fred worked for the Greek Red Cross, doing relief work for Greeks made homeless by the Turks. In 1899 the household, still with Maggie (and largely for her sake) moved to a rambling, red brick house called Tremans, near Horsted Keynes in Sussex. After his father's death, Fred had promised to live with his mother, but he found Tremans too isolated and felt rather stifled in a house full of women. After he had spent a somewhat discontented year there, his mother released him from his promise, and he took a flat at 102 Oakley Street in Chelsea and became a professional writer, eventually joined the Bath and Garrick Clubs and became quite a man-about-town. Life was very pleasant, with endless socialising and travelling about—both Hugh and Arthur thought him a "frivolous dilettante"—and sporting activities. In his youth he was good at lawn tennis, rugby, squash and curling, he skied and he was acknowledged to be perhaps the best ice-skater in the difficult English Style, gaining a gold medal from the National Skating Association. Two of his lesser-known books are his *English Figure Skating* (1908) and *Winter Sports in Switzerland* (1913). But as Maggie's condition deteriorated, it was he of the family who continued to visit her and take her on outings and generally do what he could for her. At the same time, Arthur too began to suffer from the family depressions. He had been a master at Eton for many years, and then moved to

Cambridge, first as a Fellow and later as Master of Magdalene College. All the while he wrote obsessively, a stream of pious, sentimental books and a massive diary of four and a half million words. He, like the rest of his family, never married and enjoyed romantic friendships with members of his own sex. Just as Maggie became obsessed with their father, and depressed after his death, so Arthur now involved himself in a biography of Maggie, and this took a hold on his mind from which he suffered almost continuously for the next six years, and then on and off until his death in 1925: he died on June 16th, the same date his mother had died seven years previously, and coincidentally on what would have been Maggie's birthday. Fred was the member of the family who suffered least from these destructive black depressions, although he was subject to occasional bouts, especially during his last two years or so. However, they were apparently more the natural result of his physical suffering than the disabling mental or nervous disorders of the others.

In 1914, Fred was still leading his well-ordered and agreeable life, which consisted of his writing, music, part of the summer in still unfashionable Capri, August probably in Scotland, and winter sports usually in Switzerland. In between there were visits to friends and to his mother at Tremans. But suddenly the war put paid to that whole era of security and prosperity which had seemed to the Bensons and their social equals as though it would last for ever. He took up war work in London, and Hugh died of pneumonia that October. It was Fred who made all the arrangements (following complicated instructions due to Hugh's fear of being buried alive) and he had the same melancholy task in 1918 when his mother died, waiting another year before clearing the massive family accumulations of many decades from the over-furnished Tremans. Sometime in the war years (possibly in 1915) Fred moved from Oakley Street to 25 Brompton Square, and shortly after that he began to become seriously involved with Lamb House in Rye.

2 Lamb House—a short history, before the Bensons lived there

Lamb House was built by James Lamb in 1722–3, incorporating parts of a much earlier building into the structure. The existing property consisted of three smaller houses, various outbuildings, a 'deese' for drying herrings, with a brewery occupying the later walled garden. James Lamb built an elegant red brick fronted Georgian house with a high canopy over the door, and he carried on the business of vintner, using the brewery. He was mayor of Rye thirteen times, starting not only a family tradition, but a tradition for subsequent inhabitants of Lamb House, including E. F. Benson and his own Lucia.

In January 1726, George I's ship was driven ashore at Camber Sands in a dramatic storm. James Lamb rode to meet him and brought him back to Lamb House; subsequent heavy snow forced the king to stay for four nights. On the night of his arrival, James's wife, Martha, gave birth to a son, and two days later the baby was baptised George, with the king as godfather.

In 1743 another of James's sons, John, gave a dinner party on board the customs ship which was moored off the Fishmarket. His father set off, despite the fact that he felt unwell, but saw his brother-in-law, Allen Grebell, outside his own house opposite, and asked him if he would go to the dinner in his place. To save Grebell fetching his cloak, James lent him his own red mayoral cloak. At about midnight when Grebell was returning through the churchyard, he felt a couple of heavy blows in the back. He managed to get home and told his servant he thought a drunk had collided with him and he would just recover himself by the fire before going to bed. Meanwhile that night James repeatedly awoke from vivid dreams in which his dead wife begged him to see if Allen, her brother, were in trouble. By dawn he felt so uneasy that he went across to Grebell's house, where Grebell was found sitting dead in the chair in the sitting-room, still wearing James's cloak and surrounded by a pool of blood. It was then learned that Breads, who owned the Flushing Inn and a butcher's shop in the yard, had been shouting in drunken triumph through the streets: "Butchers should kill Lambs!" He had long borne James Lamb a violent grudge (as Chief Magistrate, Lamb had fined him for giving short weight) and the previous night had lain in wait for him behind a tombstone. Seeing a man in Lamb's distinctive cloak, Breads leapt out and stabbed him with his butcher's knife. He was hanged on the Salts and his body chained to a gibbet—the remains of his skull are now in Rye Town Hall. In about 1930 E. F. Benson held a *séance* in the Garden Room and the medium, who claimed never to have heard of the murder, saw the hunched figure of a man in a cloak in the very cane-bottomed chair in which Grebell is believed to have died—it is said that the chair was given to James Lamb as a memento of his brother-in-law and he put it into the Garden Room, which had been recently built as a small banqueting room.

In 1756 James died and left Lamb House to his eldest surviving son, Thomas, who in turn became mayor 20 times before he died in 1804. It was let to various tenants until 1819, when Thomas's second grandson, the Rev. George Augustus Lamb, inherited it, and he and his brothers alternated as mayor for many years. George's son finally sold Lamb House to a banker called Francis Bellingham, who himself became mayor before dying in 1897. Bellingham's son was more interested in the Klondike gold rush in Canada than in living in Rye, and so the house came to be leased.

Henry James had coveted Lamb House ever since he had seen a sketch of the bow-windowed Garden Room by an architect, Edward Warren, two years before. At that time there seemed little chance that he might ever acquire it, but he had nevertheless confided his hopes to the local ironmonger, who thoughtfully wrote to inform James when Bellingham died. And James did indeed get the lease, and at "terms quite deliciously moderate". Warren supervised the few internal modifications while Alfred Parsons, a painter and landscape gardener, advised on the layout of the already flourishing walled garden, which had apricots, figs, pears and plums, and an old mulberry tree. In 1899 James was able to buy the freehold, also at a very reasonable price. He always delighted in Lamb House, furnishing it with care and entertaining his friends and relations with consideration and thoughtfulness. Visitors included H. G. Wells, Kipling, G. K. Chesterton, Belloc, Conrad, Ford Madox Ford, Gosse and Hugh Walpole, and his own brother, the philospher William James. And A. C. and E. F. Benson. It was on a visit to the Bensons at Addington that Henry James got the idea for *The Turn of the Screw* in conversation with the Archbishop. James wrote most of his later books at Lamb House, dictating them to a secretary directly on to the typewriter, while he paced up and down, occasionally fuelling her with a chocolate bar. He used Lamb House as Mr Longdon's house in *The Awkward Age* and in a ghost story called *The Third Person.* They worked in his beloved Garden Room in spring and summer and in the sunny first floor Green Room in colder weather. He loved the Englishness of it all, and during the First World War he applied for British nationality to show his solidarity with his adopted country, receiving it in 1915, and dying in London on February 28th, 1916. His nephew, Henry James Jr, inherited the house and let it furnished to an American widow. And now E. F. Benson comes into the picture.

2 Tremans, Horsted Keynes.

3 Lamb House and the Garden Room.

4 E. F. Benson at Brompton Square, 1920's.

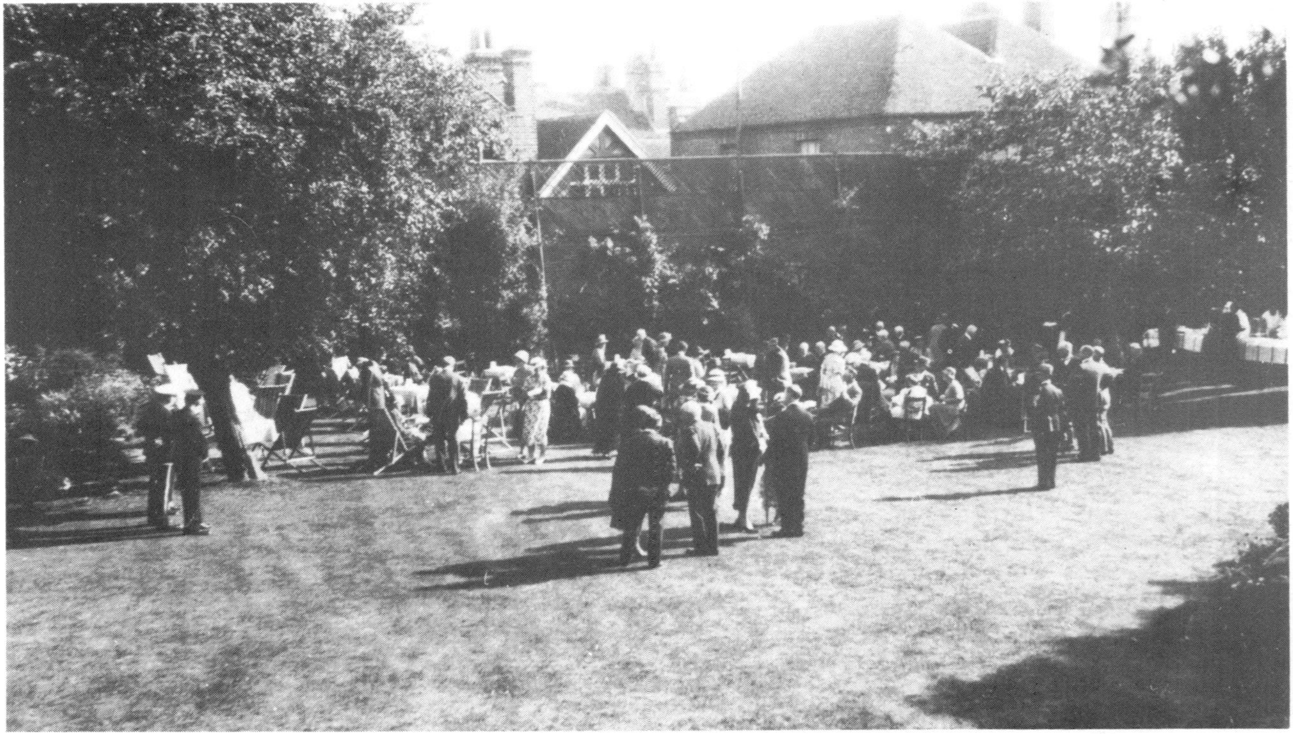

5 Lamb House garden party, date unknown.

3 E. F. Benson—an outline of his Rye years

E. F. Benson first visited Henry James at Lamb House in Rye in the summer of 1900, and his *Final Edition* opens with a detailed description of this visit. Since then he had stayed with Lady Maud Warrender at Leasam on the outskirts of Rye once or twice. Lady Maud Warrender is remembered by one Ryer as "about six foot four, bosom like a shelf, and singing 'Land of Hope and Glory' at the top of her voice"! And of course the words to that hymn were written by Arthur Benson: it became a sort of patriotic rallying-hymn in the First World War, and Elgar, who set it to music, came to hate its jingoistic connotations.

Henry James died in 1916, and some time later an American artist and friend of Fred, called Robert Norton, acquired the lease, and invited him to share the tenancy. He did this for a short time, coming down from London, where he was occupied with war work, for week-ends. Soon Norton left and offered Fred the remainder of the lease. Fred, thinking he would be spending his summers after the war at the house he shared in Capri, turned it down and passed it on to another friend. However, he then found that they couldn't renew the Capri lease and, as he had disposed of Tremans at the same time, he was happy to take over the sub-lease of Lamb House from the now departing friend from October 1919 to March 1920. He began to feel very much at home there, and found he could be perfectly content living there alone with his small household, and his writing, chess, neighbourly card games, playing the piano, birdwatching (which replaced his earlier shooting interest) and playing golf. Arthur, his brother, came and stayed twice with him, and when the lease came up for renewal later he and Fred decided to share it. They were to inhabit the house separately, so that Fred would be there in term time, and Arthur would come in university vacations with his own friends such as George Rylands, who wrote much of his fellowship thesis in the Garden Room; Arthur called Lamb House "an unspeakably delightful haven of refuge". This sharing arrangement worked out well and continued until Arthur's death in 1925, when Fred took over the entire lease which he continued to renew until his own death in 1940. Interestingly, in 1923 Arthur wrote to the vicar that he and Fred were looking for somewhere more permanent to live in Rye. Fred continued to divide his time between Rye and Brompton Square in London.

Having often had qualms about the extreme facility with which he wrote, Fred now took more serious stock of himself as a novelist, and felt that he had reached a stage where he wasn't making any progress at all, although his books still sold well. He felt he was constantly reworking the same old ground "and setting in it cuttings from my old plants", and that his characters scurried about, undergoing "stock" experiences and being bright and clever whilst the books lacked real substance. And he faced the fact that he had often used sentimentality, which he despised in others, to conceal his own lack of emotion in what were meant to be moving situations. The few early books he was not ashamed of at this stage were *Sheaves, Luck of the Vails, The Climber* and *David Blaize,* in which he had felt emotionally involved. He resolved to change direction and he turned to writing biographies and autobiographical memoirs, though this did not prevent him from "pursuing my frivolous way with the preposterous adventures of Lucia and Miss Mapp, for there was nothing faked or sentimental about them." So, although the stream of undistinguished novels continued, they were interspersed with carefully researched biographies such as those of Drake, Magellan, Alcibiades, Charlotte Brontë, Edward VII, and Queen Victoria; a number of books on his family life; more of his powerful supernatural short stories; and what we now know to be his real masterpieces, the hilarious *Mapp & Lucia* novels, which were published between 1920 and 1939, four out of the six being set in Rye. Although he certainly used some characteristics of Rye inhabitants in the *Mapp & Lucia* books (such as their animated talk as they jostled each other with their marketing baskets in shop doorways), he had no wish to mock his new neighbours and friends "of whom neither the remotest sketch or caricature ever sullied the topographical accuracy of Tilling", as he wrote later. Direct inspiration is more often taken from his earlier friends and acquaintances—see the Tilling pages at the end of this book. However, as you will see from the map in that section, the Tilling of the novels is, with very little artistic licence, Rye in almost every detail. Lamb House becomes Mallards, Tilling is named after Rye's River Tillingham, and virtually every topographical reference is based on a Rye counterpart, although whether later Tilling enthusiasts have deduced these correctly remains the subject of endless discussion.

In 1920, Fred was awarded the MBE "for services as the Honorary Secretary of Lady Sclater's Fund for Wounded Soldiers and Sailors". It was possibly really for his work as a King's Messenger.

Painful arthritis of the hip began to bother him almost as soon as he came to Rye and put an end to most of his sporting activities, apart from an occasional swim or a gentle walk on the marshes. In *Final Edition* he describes with delightful humour his futile but zealous round of both doctors and quacks, and the extraordinary treatments he underwent in a desperate attempt to be cured. There were radio-active injections and pads, taking the waters, extraction of teeth, the wearing of a crystal necklace, inoculations and iodine, Christian Science and oranges, but nothing helped. He fought self-pity but determined to avoid too many large social gatherings, preferring quiet meals with friends. He continued his passion for collecting with renewed interest as his other activities waned; anything unusual might attract him—Salopian china, old silver, or an attractive statuette in an antique shop. He also created his beloved Secret Garden, within the seclusion of its high walls, an unpretentious garden with grass, forget-me-nots and tulips, daffodils and narcissi, anemones, wall-flowers and aubretia. There was crazy paving and a small open-sided wooden summer-house. Cream roses and clematis grew against the garden walls. In the centre was a marble bust of Augustus on a brick plinth. And here he came and wrote whenever it was warm enough, or simply sat in the sun. Friends who were staying with him were allowed to sit there too, but otherwise he was undisturbed.

Fred found he quite enjoyed growing old in Rye, which he admitted he had come to love more than any other place in which he had ever lived or stayed. By now he was living in Rye for most of the year, but still spending his summers in London. He gave two very fine stained glass windows to the parish church (see separate account) and he donated a belvedere or look-out platform at Hilder's Cliff, at the end of the High Street, and a shelter beneath it. In 1933 he was appointed a J.P. or magistrate and he set about learning what was involved with his usual enthusiasm. But Fred was completely unprepared when, just at a time when he was feeling rather stale, he was elected Mayor of Rye in 1934, even though he was not on the council—the first man outside the council to take the office of mayor for forty-five years, so a great honour. It was an astonishing coincidence, because Lucia was about to become Mayor of Tilling in a new novel he had written but which hadn't yet been published. He accepted with alacrity and invited an old friend, Mrs Jacomb-Hood, to live with him "in municipal sin" or in other words to be his mayoress. He was twice re-elected, remaining mayor until 1937, and he took great pleasure in all the pomp and ceremony. The office of Chief Magistrate accompanied that of mayor, and his mayoral duties included much of the organisation of the local celebrations for George V's Silver Jubilee and later for the Coronation of George VI and Queen Elizabeth. A plaque in the fire station (in Ferry Road) records the fact that it was "officially opened on the 26th July, 1937, by the Right Worshipful, The Mayor of Rye, E. F. Benson Esq. MBE, J.P.", just after his 70th birthday. He was elected Speaker of the Cinque Ports in 1936, in time for the installation of the new Lord Warden, Lord Willingdon, at Dover. By this time he was only leaving Rye for short holidays.

When, in 1936, he was asked to contribute a couple of recipes to a local booklet, a compilation of residents' favourite dishes, his sense of humour as usual got the better of him:

A Simple Recipe
Cod à la bourgeois

Many housewives consider boiled cod to be a very tasteless sort of dish, but if prepared according to the following simple and inexpensive recipe it will be found a very nice addition to the ordinary bill of fare in case of a friend dropping in to dinner unexpectedly.

Take a slice of cod sufficient for (say) 3 persons and boil in the ordinary manner in slightly salted water.

While this is cooking, strip the flesh of 2 hen-lobsters, omitting the roe, and cut into small dice. Fry lightly in the best olive oil and set aside. Melt 1 ounce of Danish butter in a small saucepan, and when it is at foaming point add to it a heaped-up tablespoonful of Russian caviare, stirring well to prevent it clinging to the sides of the saucepan. When thoroughly mixed take it off the fire and plunge into it a bouquet of bay-leaf, mint and spring onions previously soaked in Tarragon vinegar. Add a small wineglass of Château Yquem and half that amount of old brandy, 12 heads of asparagus, ½ pint of cream and a handful of fresh truffles (if these are not procurable mushrooms will do, though the delicacy of the flavour is slightly impaired). Add pepper, salt, mustard, 1 clove and a sprinkling of nutmeg according to taste and bring to the boil. Remove the bouquet and add the 2 diced hen-lobsters, stirring well. Reduce the whole till it is of the consistency of treacle and pour it over the boiled cod. Garnish with parsley, bergamot and a few stoned olives. Squeeze over it the juice of 1 Tangerine orange and serve very hot.

Pancakes à la Borgia

Procure a small piece of glass (any broken window will serve) about 1 inch square. Pound this in a mortar till its consistency is of the finest dust, and thoroughly mix it with 6 or 8 times the amount of sifted sugar. Take 3 berries of deadly nightshade (belladonna), mince well and add one $\frac{1}{4}$ ounce of foxglove seed (digitalis), a dessertspoonful of weedkiller (arsenic) and mix together in sufficient jam or honey to neutralize the taste of the other ingredients. Spread this mixture over the surface of an ordinary pancake, roll it up in the usual manner, and sprinkle thickly on the top the powdered glass and sugar. Pass a salamander over it till the glass and sugar assumes the appearance and texture of caramel.

N.B.—Digitalis and belladonna may be procured from any chemist, but they are not always fresh, and it is wiser for this and other reasons to pick these ingredients yourself. It is also advisable, when serving an enemy with this delicious dish, to explain that you never eat sweets yourself but that this pancake is prepared according to an old family recipe.

(From *A Cargo of Recipes,* in aid of Rye, Winchelsea & District Memorial Hospital)

In 1938, he was made Honorary Fellow of Magdalene College, Cambridge, where his brother Arthur had been Master, and in this Fellowship he succeeded Rudyard Kipling and, before him, Thomas Hardy. And in the same year Rye gave him the Freedom of the Borough, and so he was made guest of honour in a final splendid ceremony at which he was presented with a silver model of Henry VIII's flagship, the *Mary Rose,* the same ship which was raised in the 1980's. The model will have been based on the only existing portrait, which is in the Anthony Roll in the Pepys Library in Cambridge, and was probably meant to be used as a container for port or wine. There was believed to be a slight local connection with the *Mary Rose* as it was thought that she was the first ship to be fitted with cannon, and that the iron for these came from Sussex foundries. However, John Munday of the National Maritime Museum thinks the first ship to take cannon was another *Mary.* In any case, the silver model was a very handsome one and joined Fred's other much-loved model ship, the *Golden Hind.*

E. F. Benson died of cancer of the throat on February 29th, 1940, and was buried in Rye Cemetery, just outside the town, having written around 100 books. About 70 of these were novels.

E. F. Benson's Funeral, St Mary's Parish Church, Rye, on Tuesday, March 5th, 1940

(Details taken from the *Sussex Express and County Herald*, March 8th, 1940)

The funeral was conducted by Dr G. K. A. Bell, Bishop of Chichester, assisted by the curate of Rye, Rev. John Hurst (in the absence of Prebendary John Fowler, the vicar and E. F. Benson's old friend). The organist and choirmaster was J. Charles Williams and he played Bach's Toccata and Fugue in D minor and his Fantasia and Fugue in G minor, as well as 'Sleepers Awake', Handel's Largo and Mendelssohn's 'O Rest in the Lord'. The hymns were 'Jesu, lover of my soul' and 'O God, our help in ages past', and Psalm XVIII and the Nunc Dimittis were also sung.

The chief mourners were a cousin, Mrs Stewart McDowall (who also represented her three sons on active service overseas), various Esdaile cousins and a cousin called Miss Sidgwick. Miss de Hochepied Larpent also represented her sister Mrs Reta Jacomb-Hood who was ill, and the Town Clerk, an old friend, Captain Edwin P. Dawes, was there, as well as Mr Benson's servants, Charlie Tomlin, Rose Edwards, Ivy Green, and George Eaton, the gardener.

There was a mayoral and civic procession to the church, and there was a number of civic mourners. Others present in the church included Mr P. Ashburnham (representing Lord and Lady Davenport), Lady Maud Warrender, Mr E. R. Pigrome, the Misses Dowling (representing the Rye Literary Society), Mrs H. C. Burra, Miss Fowler, as well as representatives of many local organisations.

The interment was at Rye Cemetery and many friends gathered in the streets as the cortège passed. His grave there is number 6223, and the inscription on the stone reads:

> 'Here lies Edward Frederick (sic) Benson M.B.E., J.P., fifth child of Edward White Archbishop of Canterbury and Mary Benson, who died on 29th February 1940 aged 72 years. Author, scholar and historian. Freeman of Rye. Three times mayor of Rye. Fellow of Magdalene College, Cambridge.'

4 E. F. Benson's private life

Since the revival of interest in E. F. Benson, in the late 1970's and '80's, virtually every biography, article, review or introduction, has stated as a fact that he was a practising homosexual. No real evidence is ever given for this, only his strange family background and that he never married and was probably more attracted to men than to women; his accounts of romantic friendships between schoolboys in his novel *David Blaize* are sometimes cited as "proof".

It can never now be *proved* either way, and nowadays it wouldn't matter one bit if he was, but it does seem to be forgotten when he is so blithely labelled as an active homosexual that, apart from the completely different moral climate, it would have been dangerously illegal in his lifetime. And perhaps, looking at it from today's context, the wrong conclusions have been drawn (or leapt to) from his writing? So, although we repeat that it can never now be *known* for certain whether he was or he was not, we are setting down what seems to us evidence which implies it was unlikely. If only to redress the balance.

Fred wrote with complete frankness in *Our Family Affairs* (1920) of the intense platonic friendships of his schooldays, in an attempt to break the existing taboo on the whole subject. Of the shameful secrecy surrounding the expulsion of two boys, he wrote: "But in heaven's name, why could we not all have been given clean lessons in natural history?" and that boys "should be taught cleanness by their elders, instead of being left to experimentalize in dirtiness . . . nothing can prevent boys from seeking to learn about those things which their elders cover up in a silence so indiscreet as to be criminal." At the time of this school scandal, he didn't understand the cause. Later he writes of "a certain emotional affection towards the coevals of their own sex which is natural to public school boyhood . . . naturally there is danger about it . . . and this strong beat of affection may easily explode into fragments of mere sensuality, be dissipated into mere 'smut' . . . But promiscuous immorality was, as far as I am aware, quite foreign to the school [Marlborough] . . . to suppose that this ardency was sensual is to miss the point of it and lose the value of it altogether . . . to confuse it with moral perversion, as the adult understands that, is merely to misunderstand it." Then again he writes of the self-imposed discipline of the dormitories: "The decency, the morality, the discipline that result from such a system, where these virtues are the result of public opinion, are of far more robust quality than if they are merely the forced product of the fear of detection." His own moral principles seem unequivocal here—cleanness and dirtiness, morality and immorality—and this concerns the time when his own emotions were at their strongest. They are reinforced in *As We Were* (1930) when he writes in even stronger words of "the slime of intemperance and perverted passions" which destroyed Oscar Wilde on his release from prison, and this in a passage generally sympathetic to a man he liked and in many ways admired.

Sir Steven Runciman, who knew him well from the 1920's, is convinced that Benson remained virginal, and indeed seemed to have a "fastidious distaste for physical contact", and while having many good friends of all ages and both sexes, he doesn't seem to have been deeply involved emotionally with anyone. Sir Steven doesn't feel that passion, either physical or emotional, played a part in Fred's adult life and that perhaps that shows in his books. (Fred said much the same thing in *Final Edition*). He thinks that Fred "probably was more attracted by young men than by young women, but it was a very innocent attraction." Unlike some of Fred's contemporaries, "he quite clearly had no desire to paw young men"—and as an extremely good-looking young man (immortalised by an admiring Cecil Beaton), Sir Steven would surely have known.

And those who would have known all there was to know about Benson in his later years were the members of his small household in Rye, and both Charlie Tomlin and Ivy Robbins were quite adamant that he was not a homosexual.

It seems highly likely that this quotation from Fred's *Travail of Gold* (1933), if one substitutes 'he' for 'she', probably sums up his own attitude fairly closely: "It was quite true . . . that she delighted in the company of young men, but as for [the] notion . . . that she laid siege to their moral rectitude, nothing could have been falser . . . She liked young men because they were, if of the right sort, pleasant to look on and lean and clean in movement, but to have been embraced by one would have caused her agonies of outrage and embarrassment."

It is hardly to be wondered at that none of the Benson children was able to enjoy normal, heterosexual relationships when one considers their upbringing. It was a classic case of the overbearing father and the perhaps over-loving, over-demonstrative mother, who was a strong personality. Was it quite normal, even in those days, for a mother to be writing to her adult son as she did: ". . . You really are the perfectest darling in the whole wide world . . . so Goodnight dearest Fred, deliciousest Fred, my own Fred . . . I am entirely yours . . ."? And should Maggie, aged 25 and living away from home, have had to write to her mother asking meekly and rather apologetically to be told just a little about the facts of life? She admitted to being vague as to what it was she was asking about, and assured her mother that she would probably be disgusted when she knew.

Fred seems to have channelled his energies into his writing, his zest for living in general, and, until his later years, into reaching the top in a wide variety of sports.

5 Benson Windows in St Mary's Parish Church, Rye

Fred had been deeply affected and impressed by a particular window in King's College Chapel, Cambridge, when he was at university, and he chose to commemorate his brother Arthur and later his parents by giving stained glass memorial windows to the parish church in Rye.

First of all, in 1928, he and Arthur's patron donated a Benedicite window in the south transept, to the memory of Arthur. He felt the jewel-like colours achieved a richness which was perhaps unique in a modern window, and he had tried to emulate the windows of Chartres Cathedral in the effect of brilliant glass mosaic in which are set round medallions depicting all manner of things created—the sun, moon and stars, the lightnings and seas, and the green things upon the earth, the whales, beasts and cattle, and the fowls of the air. Among these Fred had an avocet included, in memory of one he and his manservant, Charlie Tomlin, saw at Salthouse, Norfolk, in August 1922, which was the first to be seen there in 100 years and attracted crowds of bird-watchers. Fred wrote of this to his friend, Canon Fowler, and continues: "a friend went and shot it. I hope that when he dies he will be chained, like Prometheus, in a muddy marsh, and that an Avocet will stand by him and peck out his teeth and toenails." Arthur for some reason had bought a mountain in Cumberland, and this too is represented in the window. Arthur is shown in red academic robes in the bottom right-hand corner, near the Benson arms, and the figures of Archbishop Benson, Archbishop Davidson and a third, unknown priest are also depicted. The inscription reads: 'When I wake up after thy likeness I shall be satisfied with it. To the glory of God and in dear memory of Arthur Christopher Benson this window was dedicated, by Eugenia Langdon of Nottbeck and Edward Frederic Benson A.D. 1928.'

After lunching at Lamb House, Lord Davidson, Archbishop of Canterbury, unveiled the window and after that ceremony the Archbishop was given the Freedom of the Borough; as they talked of its privileges and customs, and as Fred watched the splendid mayoral procession from Lamb House to the church, he little realised that he himself would one day be receiving the same honour and walking (or by then, as he said, "hobbling") behind such a procession. Not long afterwards Queen Mary brought her small granddaughters (now Queen Elizabeth and Princess Margaret) to see the window.

Then, in 1937, Fred gave the West Window in memory of his parents. The design was largely his own, and he describes in *Final Edition* how the idea for it had come to him when he was sitting in a sunny corner of the Secret Garden just before Christmas 1936. He was looking at a pear tree, and the irregular patches of blue sky between its bare branches reminded him of glass in the tracery of a decorated window. Just then a dazzling white seagull passed behind the branches and through the blue segments, and then it came to him that his window would contain a host of angels swooping down through a sky of morning glory blue and alighting on the roof of the stable—the theme of the window was to be the Nativity. He couldn't himself draw, but he attempted to sketch what he visualised, and he got down the design he wanted, even though some of the angels looked like moths and others like aeroplanes. Mr Hogan, who had designed the A. C. Benson window, was also the artist of this one, and both were made by James Powell & Sons. Sixteen blues were mixed before Fred was satisfied with the exact shade of morning glory, a flower which had tangled over the wall of the house he had shared in Capri, and which now sprawled over the entrance to the Secret Garden. Charlie Tomlin is depicted as the shepherd with Taffy, the beloved black collie which had died in 1936 and was missed by the whole household. E. F. Benson is shown as a tiny figure in red mayoral robes at the bottom righthand corner and the Benson arms are at the opposite corner.

This window too was unveiled by an Archbishop of Canterbury, by this time Dr Lang, and also present was Lord Willingdon, the new Lord Warden of the Cinque Ports. Fred, as mayor, headed a civic procession from Lamb House (where his distinguished guests had lunched) to the church, and there was a separate Archbishop's procession of clergy, and it was all very splendid and colourful. The service, although it was July, resembled a December service, with 'Hark, the Herald Angels sing' and the Christmas lesson: this was in keeping with the theme of the window. The organ music before and after the service included a Bach fugue in G minor and Bach's Toccata and Fugue in D minor; this last was also to be played at Fred's funeral.

Fred also gave the church a pair of large brass candlesticks. Ivy Robbins, who was his housemaid, remembers it had been her job to clean these with brass polish when they stood in the dining room at Brompton Square, and says, perhaps a little ruefully, that they were lacquered before they were given to the church. Fred and Charlie Tomlin went to see them in their new place and they looked so handsome there that Fred said he was almost sorry to part with them.

There is no window to commemorate E. F. Benson, but there is a memorial tablet on the choir stall where he usually sat, on the south side of the chancel: 'In remembrance of Edward Frederic Benson who passed away on the 29th of February 1940. Servant of God—brave sufferer, author, three times mayor of Rye. Friend to this Church and Town.'

Part II
Charlie Tomlin's memories

1 Charlie's Early Years

It was in 1978 that we first met Charlie and Rose Tomlin through Geoffrey Prentice. Charlie was only too happy to talk about Mr Benson and his time with him, and one of us used to visit his house at 99 Udimore Road on Friday mornings for several weeks, first of all with a notebook and then a tape recorder. It is these recordings which form the substance of this section, and any quotation which is not attributed in the text is Charlie speaking. Charlie was Mr Benson's manservant in his Lamb House years, and Rose Edwards, as she then was, was his cook. After Benson's death in February 1940 they married in April and honeymooned in Brighton. Charlie did ARP work in the war, and worked as a painter for Burnhams, the Rye builders. Exactly when he started with Burnhams and when the Tomlins bought 99 Udimore Road is not clear, but William Carey remembers that from the mid 1940's onwards that was where he worked and where he lived.

William Carey and Charlie came together through the Rye Bonfire Boys which was started up again after the war, and of which Charlie became Treasurer in 1952 and William Carey Vice Chairman in 1953, then Chairman in 1954, a partnership which lasted for twenty years until they resigned together in 1973. The Rye and District Bonfire Society put on a really splendid show every November 5th with tableaux and bands, torchlight procession, a magnificent professional firework display on the Salts and a gigantic bonfire with boat burning and bloaters cooked in its ashes, the eating of which made you a "Bonfire Bloater Boy". Throughout the year fund raising events were held to pay for the large costs involved. One of these was the delivery of parcels in Rye at Christmas by Father Christmas in full rig. Charlie was Father Christmas for many years and as Father Christmas he switched on the Christmas lights in Rye and processed through the streets.

Charlie loved all this, all the dressing up and being involved in general. William Carey says he was always one to roll his sleeves up and get down to the job in hand. He took all these activities very seriously but he also had an eye for the ladies, though he was never less than the perfect gentleman. It wasn't only the Bonfire Society he worked for but also the Conservative Club when it was in the old Grammar School in the High Street (Charlie regarded the billiard table and its proper maintenance as his special preserve), and later the Rye Club in Market Road. Rose took her part in all these activities and did a lot in the Women's Institute as well. It was Charlie though who baked all their bread. Neither of them seem to have been bystanders or just customers; they were always in the middle doing things to help everything go with a swing.

Charlie retained his birdwatching interest and his golf right through his life. He retired from Burnhams in 1972. When we met him he appeared very hale and bright but he was to die suddenly in 1981. Rose was shattered by his death and she only lived another two years after him. There was a funeral service for Charlie in Rye Parish Church where he is pictured still as the shepherd in the West window. His ashes were scattered on Rye Golf Course.

Charlie was born in 1902 at Ayot St Lawrence. He said he didn't know which event had made Ayot St Lawrence more famous, George Bernard Shaw living there or his being born there. His father was a gardener with five children, but he died when Charlie was only thirteen and left his widow with the children to support. It happened that the 'boy' employed by Mrs Benson at Tremans was leaving and so she approached the school for a replacement. Charlie was next in line and also the sooner he was earning, the more help he could be to his mother. So he left school a year early and "went to Tremans as 'boy' and lodged with the coachman and thoroughly enjoyed myself, half a crown a week and my keep." The teachers at Charlie's school were a couple who were both past teaching and past their pension time but who stayed on because of the war. As soon as he left a new young man came as schoolmaster bringing innovations such as homework, "things I'd never dreamed of and I missed my chance, you see."

His father's employers came from Clifton in Bedfordshire in about 1910 to Keynes Place and built a gardener's cottage in which the Tomlin family, who apparently came with them, were installed until the father's death in 1915. His father had worked in nurseries before his gardening job and as a young man had been a steward on ships going to Australia. A strange incident to a small boy stuck in Charlie's memory about this time. The lady of the house was intensely curious as to what Mrs Tomlin was going to do, because of course she would have to leave the cottage. Charlie was asked to go up to the house and see the lady, in his not very smart but only suit. She asked him to find out what his mother was going to do, and she would give him a new suit.

When he told his mother this story she said: "If you go near that place, I'll wring your neck." So Charlie didn't go back and a new gardener came who lodged with the Tomlins for a while. Charlie had this touching memory of him. "To get from the house to our cottage we used to walk across the field; and this man was something like my father, and he done exactly the same thing, crossing with his jacket on his arm, and you could swear it was my father. I remember my mum cried looking at him."

Charlie's mother moved into the village with the family and got various jobs. At some stage she married again and had another boy. She worked in munitions in London during the first war making shells, and lived to be eighty-two. Charlie's elder brother pretended he was older than his sixteen years and joined up in the war, so that was two less to support.

Charlie was very happy at Tremans. The cook and he were "the greatest of friends". She was known as Mrs Taylor although she was not married, this being the custom for senior female servants. So with her on his side and being looked after extremely well by the coachman and his wife, "very, very nice people", his fortunes were improving. The coach was a very real mode of transport still in 1915, and Mrs Benson did not have a car. As Tremans was some distance from the village of Horsted Keynes, it must have been in frequent use. Visitors coming to stay at Tremans were met at Horsted Keynes station two and a half miles away.

Among Charlie's duties were cleaning silver, cleaning shoes, cleaning knives, and bringing food to the table for staff meals. He used to polish the oak floor every day. The method for cleaning silver was to mix Goddards powder with methylated spirits, rub this on the silver with the fingers and a brush for the crevices, wash it in very soapy water and finish off with a leather for the final polish. The washing stage was often left out. Mrs Benson had two salvers on a stand, one of which had a curious mark. This mark Charlie could remove with his finger polishing but it would always have returned by the next cleaning.

Shoe cleaning was done by putting the polish on with a brush, taking it off with a second brush and polishing with a duster. The instep had to be cleaned as well and every now and then the laces would be taken out to be washed and ironed, especially for the ladies' shoes.

Another of Charlie's tasks was to take the mail to the village two miles away and to collect it from the village as the postman did not come out so far. Apart from the cook there was a kitchen maid, a house maid, a lady's maid and a parlour maid. The parlour maid was Spicer who later came as housekeeper to Lamb House. There was only one horse for the coachman to look after. When he was needed they'd go outside and blow a whistle, but one of the two parrots (Matilda no doubt as mentioned in *Final Edition*) learnt to imitate this and frequently summoned him on false errands.

Every morning there were prayers for the servants with Mrs Benson presiding and Miss Tait playing the organ. Charlie had been a solo treble in Horsted Keynes church choir, so he was well equipped for this experience. (Mrs Tomlin said at this point, "You ought to hear him sing now!") The choir mistress used to send him a Christmas card every year for fifty years and she wrote to him on Mr Benson's death. The worship at Tremans consisted of a hymn to begin and to finish with, and of prayers and readings from the Bible in between, lasting about fifteen minutes.

Charlie said Mrs Benson was "a lovely person. Snow white hair and always had a sort of lace cap on top. Just like Queen Victoria. On the shortish side, absolutely charming—she treated me more or less as a grown-up and as nice as pie. And Miss Tait as well. Miss Tait wasn't quite so lovable, but she was an awfully nice person." Mrs Benson left the running of the house mostly to the staff. There would occasionally be guests to meals from the surrounding countryside within driving distance, and a fair amount of people who stayed there. Mrs Benson and Miss Tait constantly used terms of excessive endearment when talking to each other, "my dearest Lucy" and so on, to an extent that Charlie said was quite unusual.

Mrs Benson died in 1918 and Fred Benson's manservant was called up for armed service. Charlie was only sixteen when the household at Tremans broke up and Mr Benson asked him if he'd like to take the place of his manservant when he left for service. Mr Benson had been a fairly frequent visitor to Tremans but Charlie could not remember that he ever took any notice of him or spoke to him very much. Charlie was friendly with his manservant who was only just eighteen himself which was why he'd been called up. Charlie thought his life was highly desirable although the man himself was not so keen and was not going to return to the same work after his soldiering. Charlie said "I was very pleased when I was asked." He pointed out that men were scarce at that time and that he was to hand and convenient, when asked why Mr Benson settled on him.

There were three months to fill in and Charlie was sent to Lambeth Palace, where Archbishop Davidson was currently the Primate, to train. There was no room for him at Brompton Square where Mr Benson had his town house, until the other man left. Charlie remembered Archbishop Davidson as a visitor to Tremans. He acted as server to the Archbishop when he celebrated Holy Communion while staying at Tremans, presumably in Horsted Keynes Church. Charlie found the Archbishop's mode of celebration rather odd, "everything so ordinary and so plain."

This was because the vicar at Horsted Keynes had been very high church and had accustomed him to a very elaborate ritual. This vicar visited Tremans and used to have long arguments with Mr Benson on these matters. The vicar was particularly disliked by the gardener who was very low church. Mrs Benson was not in favour of extreme high church practice. Charlie said of this vicar: "He didn't stay all that long, and then he went as a chaplain to some girls' school. He was almost a Roman Catholic. He wanted me to go to Confession. I managed to dodge that. I think it was too much for a young lad like me!"

After Lambeth Palace Charlie joined Mr Benson in his Brompton Square house to which he had moved from Oakley Street in Chelsea as described in *Up and Down* in the 'September 1915' section. In the move the grand piano got stuck in the hall where it remained for days until Mr Benson got Harrods to move it. This they did in a few minutes, putting his other removal company to shame. Charlie and he used to go down to Tremans over a long period, spending a month at a time, to clear up Mrs Benson's effects. This was left to Fred Benson and his brother Arthur took no part in it. It was a monumental task which was at last completed and the house sold to a wealthy Greek who was succeeded by Lady Mary Edgerton.

On one of these expeditions to Tremans Charlie remembered going up to the village and coming back with the news that the Armistice had been declared. This he announced to Mr Benson and Yeats-Brown who were in the drawing room, and it was only when they explained the meaning of the word that Charlie realised the war was over. Spicer stayed at Tremans looking after things until it was finally sold. This caretaker role she maintained when Mr Benson was alternating between Lamb House and Brompton Square, so that she would caretake at whichever dwelling he was not occupying.

It was in Rye that she was to die, having a stroke in Lamb House while Charlie and Rose were in London with Mr Benson. Charlie came down to Rye but she died very soon in hospital. Then Mr Benson engaged a couple to caretake in London when he was not there. The man was a taxi driver and they returned to their own house whenever Mr Benson was in town. A Mrs Page used to look after Lamb House although she did not sleep in. Charlie and Rose would always be with Mr Benson.

Of the other servants there was a girl at Lamb House when Charlie went there who stayed on with Mr Benson but was succeeded after a few years by an Irish girl who did not last long. Mr Benson came across her in the hall surrounded by mess and said "What's all this? You haven't done this, you haven't done that." "Is that so?" she said, and that was the end of her. Then Ivy Green came in 1923 and stayed for seventeen years. Rose recommended Ivy whom she had worked with in a previous job.

The gardener when Mr Benson came to Lamb House was Gabriel who lived to be eighty-seven, "a lovely old boy" known inevitably as the Angel Gabriel. He worked right up to the last few years of his life. He had a large and handsome beard and just before he died he had to go to the hospital at the Workhouse. "Some horrible Matron, first thing she did was shave his beard off, he cried and cried and cried. He'd never had a razor to his face." Gabriel had previously worked for Lady Maud Warrender at Leasam House. Mr Benson was very interested in the garden, particulary when he first took it over, though he never worked in it himself. Gabriel lodged at the Globe Inn in Military Road and had a son but no other family that Charlie knew of. When he finally gave up, his landlord at the Globe took over the Lamb House garden. According to Mrs Tomlin, Gabriel like most gardeners was very possessive over his vegetables. Mrs Tomlin would say "Come on Gabriel, I want some asparagus for lunch." "You can't have them," he said.

The original tenancy of Lamb House was shared by Mr Benson with his brother Arthur though they were rarely there together, this by design. It was a furnished tenancy so that most of the furniture throughout Mr Benson's time was that put in by Henry James, not his own. Charlie liked Arthur Benson. "Extremely pleasant he was, a thorough gentleman." When Arthur had one of his bouts of depression, Fred Benson suggested that he join himself and Charlie in a Norfolk holiday which they spent going round churches and birdwatching. On one occasion they were driving along and there was a man beside the road with a heap of flints he was chipping for use on the road. Arthur got out of the car to ask the way and when the man told him, he thanked him and raised his hat to him. Charlie told this story as an instance of Arthur's gentlemanly chivalry.

The death of Arthur Benson in 1925 left his brother with another monumental disposal problem, part pleasure such as two cellars, the Cambridge one containing three dozen Napoleon brandy 1840 and large quantities of claret, part horror such as a room the size of Charlie's front parlour absolutely full of sacks of papers. It delighted Charlie to be able to say he'd been to Cambridge. In fact he went with Mr Benson when Magdalene conferred an honorary fellowship on him. They stayed the night and Mr Benson also apparently took up his MA degree . He left his silver to Magdalene. There was some controversy with Magdalene over Arthur Benson's estate. The will had been carelessly drafted in some way so that in certain circumstances Magdalene would be in a position to call on Mr Benson for tens of thousands of pounds which would ruin him. He was not at all happy with the way the College behaved in this matter which was eventually resolved, after much wrangling in the Fellowship, so that this threat was removed.

Mr Benson was a King's Messenger in the first world war and one of his tasks was to go to Rome and find out which side the Pope was on: apparently he was pro-German. He travelled quite a bit as a King's Messenger and was offered a decoration which he declined. He was not consulted, and was quite annoyed, when he was later given the MBE.

Mr Benson said the critics missed *Dodo* when it first came out and were so cross they were only waiting for his next book to destroy it. He said it was a bad book and they tore into it. This was one of his failures and Charlie said *Ravens' Brood* (1934) also failed to please because it had "a tiny bit of sex in it." This much displeased his regular readers who wrote to tell him so.

An important part of Mr Benson's social life was weekend visiting, when Charlie would accompany him. This was mostly before they came to Lamb House permanently, after which he settled down to a more steady existence divided between London and Rye. But in Charlie's early days with him they would spend two or three weekends a month at someone's house. These weekends would usually last from Saturday afternoon to Monday morning. Charlie remembered a weekend at Holkham Hall, Norfolk, home of the Earl of Leicester whom Mr Benson would see in London; Charlie had great difficulty in finding his master's bedroom in the labyrinth but he used to make for "a sort of marble model thing of a piece of bacon" and then he was all right. Another weekend was a very big party at the Countess of Portsmouth's at Whitchurch where there was shooting. Mr Benson never took part in any shooting in all the time that Charlie knew him, but on this occasion Charlie was requisitioned as a loader because they were short. Charlie made a mess of this and handed an empty gun to his marksman who was a very rich man called Solly Joel.

He remembered another place called Down Hall where Mr Benson would play tennis. The husband of the house lived elsewhere but his lady had a replacement in residence about which there was no secrecy. This establishment ran to several footmen and large dinner parties. Charlie particularly remembered the fantastic floral decorations on the dining table provided by the gardener and assistant gardeners. And there was also a Lady Radnor near Sunningdale where Mr Benson would play golf. Another fairly frequent weekend place was a Mrs Sassoon at Stanmore. He also visited the Sassoons at Lympne. Yet another weekend was spent at Wolverton at a house lent to a lady whose name Charlie could not recall but whom they visited there and at her house in Eaton Square, "a very good friend of his". The Wolverton house had been lent her by the Abel Smiths.

When the Earl of Athlone was Governor General in South Africa, Mr Benson was invited to visit him and Princess Alice. He didn't go because "he'd be seventeen days on a ship and it would be utterly boring". He was asked a second time but again refused. But he did visit them for weekends at their house Brantwich Park in Sussex. The Princess's butler instructed Charlie in the niceties of adding "Your Royal Highness" to any reply that was made to her. There was not much for the visiting servants to do on these weekends apart from first thing in the morning running the bath, putting out the day clothes and in the afternoon the evening clothes. Charlie used to help in the pantry but refused to help at table as others did except once in an emergency at Mrs Sassoon's.

There was a delicious story from Mr Benson's staying at Lady Radnor's. He was going out and there was a footman with the butler in

E.F. BENSON : Mr. Benson remembered in Rye, and the World of Tilling. By Cynthia and Tony Reavell, with Preface by Sir Steven Runciman. Published by Martello Bookshop. £5.95

This is a fairly substantial paperback, with 20 photographs and illustrations (many not previously published). It opens with a brief biography of E.F. Benson, and a history of Lamb House. There follows the story of Benson's manservant, Charlie Tomlin, his memories of the years in London and in Rye, their domestic routine, Benson's friends and social life, his illness and his death. Ivy Robbins, Benson's housemaid from 1923 until 1940, adds her memories and ancedotes, and then a number of Rye people who remember him, such as Constance Warrender whose father, Canon Fowler was Benson's closest Rye friend: letters are quoted. Sir Steven Runciman, the distinguished scholar and historian, remembers Benson very clearly and gives his memories and impressions, and the section closes with some recollections by other non-Rye people.

The final part serves as a modest 'Companion' to the Tilling novels. Firstly a brief chapter-by-chapter listing of the events, with chronology, for quick reference. Then a Tilling map showing houses in relation to their Rye counterparts, followed by topographical descriptions and detailed explanations for the map placings. The main Tilling characters' descriptions are then gathered from the scattered novel references, and suggested origins for these and some of the situations are given. Finally there is a chapter about Benson's real fellow-inhabitants of Rye.

Available early October 1984. £5.95 plus 55p inland postage (or 65p overseas Book Rate, STERLING MONEY ORDERS ONLY) if you would like it sent. Money with order, please, to: Martello Bookshop, 26 High Street, Rye, East Sussex TN31 7JJ.

the hall. The footman got his hat and as Mr Benson was passing he said to the butler, "Doesn't old Benson want a new 'at." Next time Mr Benson visited, he said to this same footman on arrival "Well, Benson's got a new hat." Another time he got on to the top of a bus and gave a half crown piece to cover his fare. The conductor started to count out a pile of coppers for his change. "Well," he said, "I don't want all those." And the conductor said "I observe that most people can always find coppers if you give 'em a lot." He said "You're quite an observer, aren't you?"

Mr Benson had been a considerable athlete in his day. According to Charlie he was five feet ten and a half inches tall, a measurement based on the exact knowledge he would need to have of his master's dimensions for handling his clothes. Mr Benson had only one kidney, the other having been removed in an operation, and he had once had typhoid at the same time as his sister which was ascribed to watercress contaminated from a nearby laundry. He played squash, lawn tennis, and real tennis, and just missed a Rugby Blue by being injured the week before. He played golf extremely well, being a scratch player, and he was the best skater in England in the 'English style'. Charlie remembered his doing quite a few of these things when he joined him in 1918. Mr Benson was fifty and Charlie sixteen. He remembered Mr Benson visiting his mother at Tremans and cycling eight miles over to Ashdown Forest carrying his golf clubs for a game and then cycling back, quite an achievement for a man in his late forties as he then was.

The only person Charlie actually remembered him playing golf with in Rye, apart from "a crabby old boy who lived in Watchbell Street", was Humphrey Ellis. Mr Benson said that Ellis was playing the eighteenth in some competition and was told he only wanted four for the record. He promptly turned round and hit the ball in the opposite direction, apparently not wanting any records. When Charlie repeated this to Ellis, he said "That is one of Mr Benson's stories." Golf in Rye would take place mostly in the afternoon, and Mr Benson would go out to the course on the tram.

Of Mr Benson's voice, Charlie said he had "quite an ordinary voice. You could tell he was upper crust." He didn't speak loudly or use exclamations, "just level, he had quite a nice voice really." Very occasionally he would quote a little bit of Keats and he also quoted several times to Charlie some lines which lodged themselves in Charlie's mind.

"And time remembered is grief forgotten
And frosts are slain and flowers begotten."
(Swinburne from *Atalanta in Calydon*)

He said to Charlie how beautiful the language was and that it was one of the finest poems in English literature.

Charlie just came in at the tail end of Mr Benson's athletic career, going with him when he went back to Switzerland for the skating on his first visit after the war. The characteristic of the English style in skating, according to Charlie, appears to have been restraint, *e.g.* the continental way included waving your arms and legs about but in the English style you kept your arms discreetly by your side. An important feature of the figure skating was that you actually cut the figures in the ice, so that the incised line was visible afterwards. There were no special clothes for this sport, just tweeds. The skates themselves were fixed to shoes so that they were put on as a unit. Mr Benson was also a keen player at curling, a form of bowls on ice (which he describes very entertainingly in his book *Winter Sports in Switzerland,* 1913).

Charlie had a touching little story of his own when he went down to skate. Some English people were trying to form a team for curling and they were one short. One of the ladies spotted Charlie and said, "Oo, there's a gentleman over there." "Oh, he's only Benson's servant," was the reply. Mr Benson was cross when told this and another time Charlie was included. In contrast, on a separate occasion when Charlie went down to skate, the rink had only just been flooded so would not be ready for half an hour. Sir John Simon (Liberal MP and Home Secretary) said to Charlie, "You come with me," and took him to the rink at another hotel where he got permission for Charlie to skate at any time.

Mr Benson started off Charlie on skating and a Miss Gurney took him on as well, so that he passed the first test, the Bronze. Miss Gurney was a skating companion to Mr Benson and a Brompton Square lunch guest. She wore very long skirts for skating and played practically every game including golf. Charlie said she was an excellent skater and once gave him a beautiful chess set. (There is a reference in the Vidler/ Benson correspondence to two brass candlesticks sent by Miss Gurney for Rye Museum and to her offer of a seventeen pound bronze mortar of the early eighteenth century.) Miss Gurney was only one of the small party that Mr Benson either formed, or was a member of, to go winter skating.

When we said to Charlie that he finished up doing everything that his master did, he agreed and said: "He always made a point that if he was interested in something, I took it up; so we could talk about it and share my interest with his." This even extended to the piano when he asked Charlie to strike a few notes. Charlie said "I can't do that." "Go on, do it," said Mr Benson. Charlie did but was soon stopped.

Charlie remembered that on their last day in Switzerland the hotel manager gave him a bottle of wine for his lunch. Mr Benson was very apprehensive of its effect on Charlie in the high altitude and begged him not to get drunk on the journey. But Charlie did drink it!

As well as visiting Switzerland with Mr Benson for the skating, Charlie went with him for a month or more to Capri where his friend Brooks still lived. Compton Mackenzie was on the island at that time and he would join Charlie and one other in bathing expeditions. The Capri booksellers had latched on to his presence and were displaying his books, and he said to Charlie one day "Mr Benson may be the king of English Literature and all that but I'm the king of Capri." There was quite a number of English people in Capri then and Mr Benson was disappointed with it. He thought it had been spoilt compared to his prewar memory of the place. On another occasion he had a villa at Alassio on the Italian Riviera where Charlie went with him.

2 Life in Rye and London

The domestic routine in London began with Charlie running a cold bath for his master and then calling him about eight with tea. Mr Benson would get straight into the bath and then back into bed where Charlie would bring him his breakfast tray at nine o'clock. The breakfast would be bacon and egg in various permutations, toast, marmalade and China tea with milk and sugar. He would get up about ten, work till about half past twelve and then take the dog round the square for a walk. Ten to fifteen minutes on the piano were followed by lunch. Lunch would be two or three courses, usually three and always three at night with coffee. He would always have a glass or two of wine with his meal. He particularly enjoyed rice but his main demand of Mrs Tomlin was variety from day to day.

Lunch would be followed by a rest, probably a snooze, tea in the drawing room, and then a few hours' work until a hot bath, change of clothes and dinner. Mrs Tomlin said that when he was by himself in the evening: "There was one thing he always did, on his own, he always dressed for dinner, and you'd see him sit to dinner in his evening dress. Even if he was ever so tired, he changed." After dinner he would work again until about ten when Charlie would take him a whisky. Sometimes they would have a game of chess together. Charlie was allowed to smoke but didn't get any whisky. It was Mr Benson who taught Charlie chess. "He taught me to play. It must be rather tiring to teach anybody. But he done it a very smooth way. He started off by getting the positions all set up, and then leave it until I got that. And then the various opening moves until I'd got that and so on. I wasn't all that long learning."

On one occasion Mr Benson suggested that Mr Pigrome, who was a master at the Grammar School and ran the Rye Chess Club at the Rye Literary Institute in Market Road, should play Charlie in the Garden Room at Lamb House. This game was part of an all-Sussex competition, and these games were usually played in the Institute. They played with Charlie's set which was a very small ivory set no bigger than those used in travelling. Charlie won to his surprise as Mr Pigrome was a good player and Charlie did not consider himself one. But apparently Mr Pigrome was heard to complain afterwards that the set was so small he couldn't concentrate (a fact that other chess players confirm as likely, however improbable it may seem to non-players). Charlie reached the final but was defeated by the Sussex champion in Hastings on July 19th 1931.

There was a burglary once at Brompton Square during Spicer's time. She was out and they broke in through the basement door. They broke open a chest, took out all the silver and laid it all over the bedroom floor. They left the silver and only took one or two gold oddments and a pair of binoculars. On another occasion: "There was painting or something going on and ladders and things in the basement. And Rose and I had been taking the dog for a walk . . . In opening the back door the area door on the front side must have blown open. We went out, took the dog for a walk, came back and heard a noise. It was a policeman. He'd seen the door open, walked into the house and been all over the house. He said 'I'll have to report you.' We said 'If you report us, we'll report you. You've no business to be here without permission.' And he calmed down after that." But Mrs Tomlin then said with her slight Welsh lilt: "I was nearly frightened out of my life to see this policeman standing inside. I absolutely screamed." "We became friends with the policeman after that. He came and brought his girl friend to see us." "We were great friends, they used to come and call often," said Mrs Tomlin.

The main variation in routine at Rye was that Mr Benson would get up for his breakfast, and would have a walk round the garden and some talk with the gardener before settling down to his morning's work at about ten. Mrs Tomlin would take him her menu book every day and he would look to see if he'd had the proposed dish too recently. Mrs Tomlin kept a record of the guests at his dinner and lunch parties (unfortunately lost) and what menus they had, so that they would not get the same menu twice. There was much more entertaining in London than Rye, though with his pattern of a month in Rye and a month in town there was little opportunity for his London friends to ask him back. So at this period of his life he seems to have been giving rather than receiving hospitality.

In Rye he would be called at eight, shaving water brought, a cold bath run and clothes put out, and he would be down to breakfast at nine. Charlie would take him up the papers which he'd look through and would tell him about any particular movement in shares. The daily papers were the *Times* and the *Telegraph,* periodicals the *Times Literary Supplement* and *Spectator,* with probably the *Sunday Times,* all supplied by Deacons at 26 High Street which became Gouldens in 1929. Mr Benson had given Charlie a book about investment and encouraged him to save and invest which Charlie managed to do on a small scale. Sometimes Mr Benson would telephone his stockbrokers or they him. It had to be something important for him to come downstairs to use the telephone, of which he was not particularly enamoured. He would only use it for business or just occasionally for invitations, though usually telephone invitations were made by Charlie for him. The telephone would not be used for 'chat' and had a room to itself in Lamb House, the first on the right as you go in.

The panelled room opposite, through which you went to get into the garden and therefore the Garden Room, was not used except to pass through. The Garden Room was where he would spend his morning and was where he would receive any visitors. Sometimes in winter the Green Room on the first floor would be used instead. There was a grandfather clock in the hall which was lined with books on the left hand side between the first two doors. Books were everywhere in the house, even in the telephone room. Charlie used to have a go at some of the books, Pepys in particular he remembered as enjoyable. But a lot of the books he said were very highbrow or in foreign languages which he couldn't manage. But apparently Mr Benson didn't tackle these books either.

The head and bust of Rameses the Second, which Maggie Benson had excavated at Karnak and brought home, was moved from Tremans via Brompton Square to Lamb House where it was placed in a corner of the hall between the stairs and the telephone room door. Henry James's bust now stands in the hall behind the front door. Of this sculpture, Charlie said Henry James's brother had come across it, in a linen room (now a bedroom) which led to a bathroom, and had exclaimed "Oh, what a horrible thing!" He asked Charlie to get rid of it but he didn't. "You've certainly got me to thank that it's still there," said Charlie.

The banisters to the stairs were painted white and Charlie later had the terrible experience of having to remove decades of this white paint when the house was done up by Rumer Godden. He was employed by the builders she used and he told how they spent weeks with scrapers and pieces of broken glass removing the paint from these elaborately moulded banisters. "I thought it was wicked," he said. He was delighted that the paint was restored by a later tenant.

When Charlie first went to Lamb House there was no electric light. There was gas in the hall and dining room, oil lamps in the principal rooms and candles for the bedrooms. Charlie remembered how difficult it was to read in bed by candlelight. Oil lamps were effective, especially when they had the new Aladdin variety with mantles like the gas lamps.

The Rye routine would continue with writing in the Garden Room from about ten or half past ten through to half past twelve when he'd take a stroll round the streets. Then there would be a quarter of an hour at the piano followed by lunch punctually at half past one, a bit of a rest, and then a good walk outside which in the earlier years was up to two hours. But with his lameness, it got more and more curtailed, finishing up as a potter round the churchyard. Mr Benson never had a car. He used to say it was a waste of time to have a chauffeur coming in every morning to say "What are we doing today sir?" If you wanted to go somewhere, you could always hire a taxi. His lameness was caused by arthritis in his hips and started on a visit to Switzerland after the first war when he went skating. The very first day he felt a slight stiffness which he thought was temporary, but in fact it never went away for the rest of his life, only intensified. He tried skating again in Switzerland the next year but it just got worse and he had eventually to give up.

When he was working on his last book, *Final Edition,* it didn't come at all easily to him and he had great difficulty in carrying on with it. He was usually a quick and fluent writer. Once it was written, he would send it to a lady who ran a typing school. She would type it, charging him more for his bad handwriting, and then he would go through the typescript. It was at this stage that he revised and corrected. The corrected typescript then went to the publisher and later came back as galley proofs, a set of which Charlie was sometimes given for his own reading. We asked him if he was always polite about the books. "Oh yes, yes. Naturally I couldn't criticise all that much, I don't think. I liked *Ravens' Brood*—I read that in galley proof."

When in Rye he would go to church fairly regularly but not when in London. Just occasionally he went to Brompton Oratory for the Roman Catholic service although Brompton Church was next door. There was a small golf round fitted out on the lawn at Lamb House for putting. Charlie used to cut the grass. Mr Benson would quite often have a game with Charlie before lunch, "most restful periods", the results of which were fairly even until towards the end when Charlie would win more as Mr Benson "went off most things".

The piano in the Garden Room was a Bechstein and his daily practice morning and evening was often heard by the passers-by outside. He played a lot of Chopin, Brahms and sometimes even Beethoven's Moonlight Sonata of Lucia fame. Charlie said the Brompton Square neighbours may have got a bit fed up with Mr Benson's repertoire as the piano was fairly close to their wall. Mr Benson used to go to the Henry Wood Promenade Concerts and would take Charlie for company. He would ask Charlie what he had enjoyed most. Charlie's tastes were catholic but he said he "really got to enjoy it", particularly Mendelssohn. Charlie agreed that it was unusual for someone in Mr Benson's position to take his servant to concerts. They would go to the Queens Hall as well where Charlie remembered Myra Hess playing. After the concert Mr Benson would go straight home by taxi. There was also a musical show called *Immortal Hour* which he went to twice with Charlie and to which Charlie also took Rose. Charlie remembered a haunting song, 'How beautiful they are, the lordly ones . . .'

Mr Benson was a regular cigarette smoker, about twenty to thirty a day of Egyptian Number One bought from Lewis's in Broadway, Westminster. He didn't smoke cigars or a pipe, nor did he use a holder for his cigarettes. Charlie was in charge of cigarette supplies and used to buy a pound weight about every month. He dreamt once that he'd forgotten to order and couldn't think how to get the cigarettes down to Rye. He did forget once and Mr Benson had to have "some Turkish things". Charlie had two other nightmares. "One was that we was travelling somewhere and as the train was moving off the platform I looked out of the window and saw our luggage on the platform. I'd never let that happen. And the other one was that we were having a lunch party or dinner party, and I kept putting off laying the table and people arriving had to lay the table themselves."

In the late seventies at Truro the Benson family had a sheepdog called Watch who appears in the family photograph of that time. Charlie said they used to talk about Watch a lot, so he was obviously deeply loved. (Maggie Benson later had a sheepdog at Tremans called Taffy.) Mr Benson's own dogs were first Taffy and then Crown. Taffy was Rose Tomlin's dog that she came across as a puppy in Wales and persuaded Charlie to ask Mr Benson if she could bring it back. "How she got away with it I don't know but she brought it back. And of course he fell in love with it." After Taffy's death Mrs Farquharson, who lived near Perth, came to the rescue. "She got her bailiff to send a dog down, and Rose and I went to St Pancras to pick him up. Miserable thing he was, the weak one of the litter, one they said would never make a dog at all. And anyway we fed him up and he became actually bigger than his breed. We fed him on Bemax," said Charlie. "I used to wake up in the night with my alarm clock to give him brandy," said Rose. Mr Benson said Crown would have to go away to be trained because he used to go into the Garden Room and immediately cock his leg by the piano. Eventually Rose and Charlie got him trained but they didn't allow Mr Benson to send him away.

Mr Benson kept a scrapbook called *The Book of Fearful Joy.* Into this went all the photographs and caricatures that amused him. He had a collector's passion for odd photographs of the Prince of Wales whose ideas of dress he considered quite unsuitable, particularly his loud plus fours. His friend Philip Burne-Jones who was a brilliant caricaturist always included a picture of himself in abject misery in his letters to Mr Benson. Mr Benson thought the abdication of Edward VIII was "very off". "Pity my father didn't drown him," he said, as it was the Archbishop who had christened the baby prince. Charlie told the story of Mr Benson and his friend Godfrey Thomas, equerry to the Prince of Wales, both being shocked at the time of the Prince's visit to Wales when he said about the social conditions, "Something must be done!" and promptly returned to an ostentatious state banquet at Buckingham Palace. Sir Godfrey Thomas was partial to broad beans and bacon, and had to shave twice a day, "a very serious man but very nice."

Mr Benson would receive an invitation to the Buckingham Palace Garden Party. He would take a taxi to Constitution Hill, walk in and leave his card so that the Lord Chamberlain would know he'd been, walk around and out again. The point of this was that he liked to be on the list but did not want to hang around and get into a line to see the Queen. Charlie said that he was inwardly proud of his aristocratic connections, his social position and of his father having been the Archbishop of Canterbury. "He mentioned the King's College Choir and he said, 'Of course you know what makes them so wonderful is they're all gentlemen's sons—they know how to speak, they've got the right pronunciation.' He was rather keen on that sort of thing."

There was a famous visit by Queen Mary to Rye in March 1935 when she was staying at Eastbourne with King George V who was convalescing. Queen Mary was going the round of the antique shops and sent for Mr Benson to accompany her. She visited Gassons in Lion Street and what was then Delves opposite. She bought something in Gassons and indeed they still have her secretary's request for a bill. Mr Benson asked her back to Lamb House which she accepted. He rushed back saying, "The Queen's coming, the Queen's coming," for the household was in no way prepared. In fact Charlie was on his way out to play golf. "I had on a light blue jumper and I opened the door to her. I saw her give one sort of sideways glance, I expect she wondered who I was. And then she came in and walked through to the Garden Room and had a chat." She then went on to lunch at Iden with the Aubrey Smiths.

3 Mr Benson's friends and his death

Among Mr Benson's personal friends, Charlie particularly remembered Yeats-Brown and Major Archie Daukes. Yeats-Brown was a bachelor but "eventually married a Russian woman". Of Mr Benson's view of this lady Charlie said: "I don't know if he was really struck with her, but I think she was very intelligent and of course he would like that part of a person."

Charlie liked Major Daukes. The Daukeses lived at Egerton Terrace opposite Brompton Square and would come to meals with Mr Benson who "wasn't all that keen" on Mrs Daukes. He liked the conversation at table to be conducted in a civilised state of order with one person only talking at a time and everyone getting a chance of developing the topic. But Mrs Daukes would always interrupt this measured flow with something quite irrelevant which did not endear her to him. Charlie said Mr Benson enjoyed parties and company and conversation in general. He was extremely good at keeping the conversation going. His parties rarely exceeded six persons precisely because over that number conversation becomes multiple in utterance and various in subject.

It was Archie Daukes, Charlie thought, who started Mr Benson on birdwatching as he was a great enthusiast. Mr Benson kept this up from 1921 until prevented by lameness, and introduced Charlie to the pastime in which he maintained an interest for the rest of his life. The Daukeses came to live in Rye after the second world war and he then moved to Norfolk when Mrs Daukes died. Major Daukes was very distressed by her death and asked Charlie up to stay with him for a week because Charlie had known her. They would go birdwatching together and Major Daukes would keep asking Charlie about Mr Benson and Mrs Daukes. "Did he like her or didn't he like her?" Charlie rightly and kindly pretended that he did like her.

One of his oldest friends was Eustace Miles, Amateur World Champion at racquets, at tennis and at squash-tennis; and author of numerous books on diet and physical and spiritual health. They had been friends at Marlborough and then at King's College, Cambridge, and had collaborated on two bizarre publications, *Diversions Day by Day* (1905) and *Daily Training*, in Hurst and Blackett's Imperial Athletic Library. The first book is illustrated by photographs of them playing strange indoor versions of tennis and other games, and describes various exercises including those for healthy breathing. Eustace Miles was a vegetarian who opened a chain of vegetarian restaurants, and had a health food shop in Chandos Street. When he came for a meal, he would be offered vegetarian food which Mr Benson would share. Charlie said his wife (Hallie, a writer) was "the ugliest woman you'd ever seen."

Another close friend was George Plank, an artist who had a lovely house at Five Ashes in Sussex built by Lutyens who was his friend. A story was told of Lutyens visiting this project: "He came down there one day and they was putting in the glass in the downstairs lavatory. He said, 'What the devil are you doing there?' They said, 'Putting in the glass.' He said, 'Yes, but why this frosted glass?' 'It's a lavatory, sir.' 'I know it's a lavatory, but why make it look like one?'" Plank refused to have electric light in the house because he thought it vibrated and fluctuated. He preferred the steady light of an oil lamp. There was a picture of his in Mr Benson's London drawing room of a gorgeous peacock, "every tiny little feather", and he designed Mr Benson's book plate with its motif of a pierrot holding an enormous quill pen and bestriding the globe.

George Plank was also a friend of Lady Sackville, mother of Vita Sackville-West. Mr Benson went with Charlie to stay with Lady Sackville one weekend at her house in Brighton. Mr Benson and she were great friends according to Charlie, who liked Lady Sackville in spite of her being a very unusual person, remembering her as being "great fun". Vita Sackville-West he remembered as coming to Lamb House and Harold Nicolson to lunch in Brompton Square. Another lunch guest in London was Derek Verschoyle, literary editor of *The Spectator* from 1932 to 1934. Yeats-Brown also worked for *The Spectator* with great energy for many years and wrote an obituary of Fred Benson for that journal.

Dame Nellie Melba was a visitor both Charlie and Rose Tomlin remembered vividly. Once she wanted a copy of one of Mr Benson's books which he couldn't find, so she asked Charlie to help. "Do be a friend, do be a friend," she said, "and if you find one I'll send you my photograph." Charlie couldn't find one amongst the spare copies Mr Benson had upstairs but only the master copy from his collection of first editions which he kept on the "halfway landing up to the drawing room". Charlie sent this sole copy but Mr Benson never found out. He duly received the photograph and a Christmas card.

The vicar of Rye (from 1921 to 1942), Canon Fowler, was a frequent visitor. His gift of mimicry was particularly relished by Mr Benson, who didn't make any attempt in this line himself and wasn't given to extravagant gestures, but warmed to amusing theatrical behaviour in others. The Canon's most memorable imitation was apparently of the aged and extremely deaf Miss Franks, about whom there were two stories.

One was when Mrs Tomlin was taking the collie Crown for a walk and met Miss Franks, who said "I've never seen a fox on a lead before." Rose replied "It's a dog." But Miss Franks repeated "I've never seen a fox on a lead before." The second story is even richer. "Someone had just had a baby and she saw the vicar and she asked if she could have this churching ceremony and he said 'Oh yes, you come to the Clare Chapel at 6 o'clock on such and such a day.' And just before the time came Canon Fowler found he couldn't do it and he asked his new curate if he'd take the service. The curate said yes and Canon Fowler said 'She'll be in the Clare Chapel at six.' So he went along at six o'clock and he saw someone kneeling down. He said to her 'If you come up to the altar we'll have the service there.' And he went up to the altar and she didn't do anything. So he thought 'I expect her legs are bad and all that sort of thing, I'll go to her.' So he went back to where she was and read the service over her. And as it finished, she looked up and said 'What have you been doing?' Poor Miss Franks, over eighty, to be churched! And the curate, he had a bit of a nervous breakdown, he disappeared, he didn't stay very long." Who can blame the curate who'd just read over an elderly spinster a service which applies to a woman with a newly born child?

Mr Benson spent Christmas several times at Lamb House and the servants would decorate the Christmas tree and arrange the holly. His Christmas party might be four in all, usually Canon Fowler and his daughter, now Mrs Warrender. The fourth member would probably be Mrs Jacomb-Hood, widow of the artist. Charlie used to play golf with him at the Artisans Golf Club along Military Road. Mrs Jacomb-Hood was Mr Benson's mayoress and lived in The Other House in West Street. Another Rye character was a very jolly and very military Colonel Reid, whom Charlie was convinced was in *Miss Mapp* as he also thought was the Secretary of the Golf Club (Captain R. Dacre Vincent), who was somewhat abrupt in manner. Colonel Reid lived at 29 Watchbell Street which Charlie remembered clearly as he worked there when he was with Burnhams the builders. The Colonel had died and Mrs Reid, "a fussy old thing", said she wouldn't pay the bill if there was any mess. Charlie and his mate, Mr Hobbs, somehow pulled over a can of paint with a dust sheet. But they cleared it all up, put the carpet on top, and Mrs Reid never knew. There was also a Captain Bendall who was connected with the Oak House Tea Rooms. When Charlie was asked if these people did not take offence when the books came out with

6 Charlie Tomlin as a young man.

7 Gabriel the gardener.

8 Charlie Tomlin with Taffy in Lamb House garden, mid 1930's.

9 Charlie Tomlin working for Rye Bonfire Boys in the late 1960's or 1970's.

themselves caricatured, he said: "They didn't recognise themselves, but I did."

Charlie remembered a Mrs Farquharson who had a town house just opposite Mr Benson's in Brompton Square and who was always late for dinner. This used to make him absolutely furious and Charlie would have to ring her up, sometimes twice, to find out if she was coming. Once the meal had actually started to save it getting spoiled, but eventually she always turned up. "Hullo Dodo," she'd say, kiss him, and all would be well. She always kissed him goodbye, too. To his close friends he was Fred, but he was known generally as Dodo Benson. According to Charlie, Mrs Farquharson was head of the clan Farquharson and a great friend of the Duke of Kent. "She was a very nice person and during the war she went down to Reading to see her nurse and the house was hit by a bomb and she got killed."

Another friend and Lucia fan was Lady Patricia Ramsay, granddaughter of Queen Victoria. Her husband the Admiral was a great mimic as also was Miss Brougham, a gift so much appreciated by Mr Benson. Charlie remembered a lunch party at Brompton Square when Ivor Novello was a guest and they discussed the possible dramatisation of the Mapp and Lucia novels. Lady Carisbrooke, "a wonderfully nice person", was also present and was tremendously enthusiastic about the idea. (*Mapp and Lucia* and *Lucia's Progress* are both "cordially dedicated to the Marquis of Carisbrooke" while none of the other four Lucia novels have any dedication.) Charlie thought the Ramsays were also at this luncheon. Mr Benson was very keen on the project.

Beverley Nichols was a lunch guest and on one occasion he came with his nephew. This must have been the time he was contemplating his piece *E. F. Benson or very much at home* (from *Are they the same at home?* 1927), because Mr Benson asked him if he was going to show it to him before he published and he said yes. But apparently he didn't, as Mr Benson was pretty peeved at a reference in the article to his novels "growing more and more dusty on the shelves of the subscription libraries. He doesn't care, I'm sure." In fact he did. "Mr Benson didn't like that at all," said Charlie. Mr Benson had a mild dig at him in retaliation in some review of a publication where Beverley Nichols is in Italy or somewhere abroad and suddenly at the end realises it is April and the daffodils are blooming in England. So he has to rush home, of which Mr Benson wrote "I hope to God he got back in time." (Beverley Nichols was to retain a certain animosity towards Mr Benson until his own death in 1983.)

A. C. Cronin the novelist came to lunch once or twice, and then the conversation was about writing. Mr Benson did some book reviewing, particularly for *The Spectator* when Yeats-Brown had some editorial influence. Hugh Walpole used to come and see Mr Benson. And there was a publisher called Marrot who had a house in Mermaid Street he called Robin Hill, after the house of that name in Galsworthy's *Forsyte Saga.* He had once turned down Yeats-Brown's *Bengal Lancer,* which became a best seller. This publisher would argue with Radclyffe Hall in Lamb House, much to Mr Benson's amusement. Mr Benson used to say the reason *The Well of Loneliness* achieved such notoriety was that it came out in August when all society had left London: it was published on July 27th 1928. It was only a review in the *Sunday Express* damning it which brought it to anybody's notice. Without that it would have remained in decent obscurity. Probably through Yeats-Brown, Charlie thought, Mr Benson met Edith Sitwell.

When guests came the food was the same as Mr Benson would normally have but this was a very high standard anyway. "Mrs Tomlin was a very good cook: she was noted throughout society," said Charlie. Her main source was *Marshall's Cookbook.* Mrs Tomlin had a vivid memory of a visit by Dame Ethel Smyth. The pudding was meringues, nine of them, which were sent up by the hoist to the dining room. And then there was a rhythmic banging which Rose Tomlin thought was her meringues being attacked. She couldn't understand why they were so hard. In fact Dame Ethel was rehearsing her music on the table with a fork for the benefit of the company. "An awfully nice person, but very, very mannish of course," said Charlie. Dame Ethel wore ties but not trousers which would have been outrageous. No such inhibitions restrained Radclyffe Hall who lived in Rye and would come to dinner in men's evening clothes, her only concession to femininity being a frilled shirt which no man would have worn then, boiled shirts being *de rigeur.*

Mr Benson's cousin, Mr McDowall, and his wife used to come fairly frequently. He was science master and chaplain at Winchester, and Mr Benson liked him though he was not so keen on his wife. It was she who, when Mr Benson died, cleared up everything for her son who was the sole beneficiary. She came to lunch at Brompton Square once with her son whom she was trying to bring out, but he was not forthcoming (as what son would be in those circumstances?). When she was clearing up Lamb House, the dog Crown refused to go for a walk with her as she put him on a lead which he never usually had. Charlie and Rose thoroughly approved of Crown's good sense.

Another visitor to Lamb House for lunch was the Duchess of Bedford, who appears to have taken a shine to Charlie. When he went to work for Burnhams after the breakup of Lamb House, she always used to ask for him to come and do any work at her large house in Winchelsea and later at the smaller house near Brede Place to which she moved. This extended apparently to serving at table, and on one occasion to clearing up the house ready for tenants, doing her packing and virtually putting her on the train.

Charlie considered Mr Benson a good employer and said he was always very friendly to Rose and Ivy and himself. He said of Mr Benson's manner that he could sometimes be offhand but that once you knew him and he got to know you, it was quite a different matter altogether. The wages were if anything slightly under the going rate but Charlie thought he more than made up for this in other ways. Charlie's birthday was the day before Mr Benson's, so he always remembered it. Sometimes he'd give him money to go and get a suit but "it was always quite a decent present". "He'd certainly wake up one day and say, 'It's about time I give you a rise', but of course it was never very big."

"Holidays, it was rather strange, never worried about such things. Always travelling about with him, it was a holiday in itself. Because we went away, say like going to Droitwich, we spent the whole day playing golf. I went eleven years. And then one day, one year I'd heard so much from Rose about Wales that I got the idea that I'd go there. I'd got a motorbike at that time and I said I'd rather like to go for a holiday. And of course he was all for it. So I went back to Rose's home."

In fact this was the only official holiday that Charlie had in his time with Mr Benson. Otherwise he was always on duty with no regular day off, perhaps "one Sunday in two and special days but you just never worried". Charlie thought that this was unusual and that in other households there were regular holidays and days off, but that it never occurred to Mr Benson to offer or to Charlie to ask as they were both quite satisfied with the arrangements as they were. In Rye Charlie would manage golf practically every afternoon, and in London or Rye if he wanted to go out in the evening he would choose a day when Mr Benson was out to dinner. "Actually there was only two weekends in the whole time I was with him that he went away on his own, and that was chiefly because there wasn't room for me."

"In London . . . he'd got an awful habit of having a lunch party on the Saturday when I wanted to go and see football. But anyway I used to do the lunch, and perhaps I'd clear up afterwards and I'd run all the way to Stamford Bridge. Sometimes it was not possible and people didn't go on time, and he'd say 'What was the football like?' and I'd say 'I didn't have a chance, did I?'"

One of the ways Mr Benson looked after his servants was in sickness when many employers would simply send the servants home or to hospital. After only three years with Mr Benson, Charlie had a very serious bout of bronchial pneumonia, "galloping consumption" according to the regular doctor. "That was in 1921. I was eight weeks in bed, I know, and fifteen weeks altogether. And of course he was very good. At one time I had two nurses, day and night, and I don't know what came over me but the night nurse was a beautiful woman who I hated the sight of, which is most unusual. But they got rid of her actually, because I didn't like her. So they got another one. She was very old. She'd got a beard and she used to shave every day. But she was a very nice person, yes . . . And of course during the crisis there was two doctors . . . and they sent for Ma because they thought I was going to die and she stayed for a week or two."

Even more complications occurred during this illness of Charlie's. In the contract Mr Benson had for the lease of Lamb House there was a clause allowing the landlord the use of the house for one month during a certain period of time. He wanted to exercise this option and come over from America. Mr Benson held him off for quite a while but eventually Charlie had to move out to the lodgings in Ferry Road at which his nurse was accommodated. He remembered being carried out of Lamb House into an ambulance. It happened that the church bells were tolling so he said to his porters: "Sounds nice." They were shocked and told him not to think like that, assuming that he thought he was dying and being carried out for the last time.

Mr Benson paid the bills for all this and similarly when Rose was ill at Brompton Square he employed a trained nurse to look after her for about a month. "He'd always pay the dental bills and all that. Very, very kind in those sorts of ways, very, very kind."

In the last few years of his life, Mr Benson suffered from depression to which his family had been so very prone. He wouldn't show this. "He was very good with his friends. When they came to lunch, he was just as he'd always been. They'd say 'how's your legs?' and he'd say 'Oh quite all right.' But when they'd gone he'd get like that. He'd never grumble at me but he'd grumble about himself." Chiefly he'd complain about not being able to walk and do anything. "It was quite a lot to put up with the last two years, the last year especially."

Charlie thought these depressions were more marked than those normal to old age "but I think anybody coming casually to lunch or dinner, they wouldn't even know." He felt he'd come to the end and his work wasn't going as he liked. He got very apprehensive if he had to make a speech or ceremonial appearance in his public capacity and would tell Charlie he couldn't manage it. But Charlie would encourage him and everything would be all right in the end. Charlie accompanied him in his mayoral duties at all general functions though not at council or other meetings. "Of course there was really no reason why I should have gone at all but I was a sort of stick there really. He was walking with two sticks, but mostly earlier on he had just one stick. Like going to Dover and that sort of thing, I'd just walk behind him." In other words Charlie was his psychological aid whose presence obviously reassured him. Visits to Dover would be for Cinque Ports ceremonies when Mr Benson was mayor.

Mr Benson died in University College Hospital, London. Dr Gardner Hill was in charge of the case and they suspected cancer but it was not until he died that they discovered it in the tissues of his throat. He smoked about twenty to thirty cigarettes a day all the time Charlie knew him. Towards the end of his life Henry James's nephew had offered him the freehold of Lamb House but he did not take advantage of it. He said he was leaving his house in Brompton Square to his distant cousin and with Lamb House as well it would mean his unfortunate heir would have two houses and be unable to live in either. He became obsessed with money towards the end and also suffered from what Charlie called "nerve trouble". Charlie said that Mr Benson "was never really flush until after his brother died".

Charlie received a mass of letters on Mr Benson's death which were still extant when we interviewed him but have since vanished. Most of the people in Charlie's anecdotes had written and many others. There was one spiritualist and emotional lady who was excessively devoted to Mr Benson, a late admirer whom he did not take to, and who continued to send flowers on the anniversary of his death for many years. George Plank wrote "Please forgive the address on the envelope, I don't think I heard your surname." He had written on the envelope "Charles". Lady

Evelyn Lister began her letter "Mr Tomlin". Mr Benson "always had her photograph" and (unrelated information) she "was supposed to have been a bit of a gourmet". She doesn't seem to have been in any way connected with Mr Benson's friend Regie Lister. The Honourable Eleanor Brougham (born on the fourteenth of February and named Mabel Valentine, daughter of Lord Brougham and Vaux) was a long-standing friend, a neighbour in Brompton Square and a guest with her maid at Lamb House. She began her letter "Charles", and Yeats-Brown his "Dear Charlie".

The Honourable Eleanor's letter continued "I cannot realise that I shall never come to lunch in Brompton Road (sic) again." Charlie said: "After he died, she come to this house. She asked if she could come to this house. We told her we'd only got a humble one. She liked it, so that was all right." She stayed with the Tomlins in Udimore Road, Rye, bringing her maid with her.

There was a lady from Albany Villas, Hove, who saw Charlie's name in the paper and wrote "I'm a warm admirer of his books and his brilliant talent. I knew his cousin." There was a letter from Down Hall, Harlow, where they had weekended, and one from Lady Worcester who addressed Charlie simply as "Tomlin". "Lady Worcester wrote to me lots of times, she must have been in love with me, I should think." Mrs Tomlin: "She took you for a walk in the woods." Charlie: "I must tell you that she was very much older than me."

Mrs Sassoon wrote from Newmarket "My dear Friend". There were letters from Mrs McDowall and the Daukeses. Mrs McDowall wrote: "On the Thursday I should like a chicken for lunch and one guest," of which Mrs Tomlin said, "She'd put her orders down from London or from Winchester, wherever she was." This was in the period after his death when she was clearing up the estate. Charlie and Rose were left enough money for three months which was arranged through Captain Dawes. "I think if it had been left to him we should have still been there now." They were getting a bit fed up but finally, after the bombing of Lamb House, they had to get out.

Mrs McDowall wrote to Charlie that the last word she heard Mr Benson speak was his name. He murmured "Now I want Charlie . . ."

Part III
Memories of Mr Benson by others

1 Ivy Robbins

Ivy Green (now Mrs Robbins and in her early eighties) worked as housemaid for Mr Benson from May 1923 until his death in 1940, alternating between Lamb House, Rye and 25 Brompton Square in London. Her sister was at the same time cook to Clare Sheridan, one of Mr Benson's Rye Friends.

She says Mr Benson was a real gentleman, very kind and thoughtful, with a friendly disposition, a nice smile and blue eyes. "He never disputed how the household was run, if anything did cross him an apology was the answer, and then the incident was closed . . . If he was sent meat from the main butcher in the High Street (Ashbees) that was rather tough, he would go in and complain. This happened rarely. But if it was good and to his liking he would call in and praise." Together with Rose and Charlie, she tried to cheer him up when he was suffering from his arthritis—for instance they made him small iced cakes for special occasions. When he became mayor, Rose baked one, and Ivy drew the Rye coat of arms for Rose to ice over. On another occasion they made him a cake which looked like a golf course, which pleased him very much.

She remembers the two royal visits clearly. When George V was convalescing at Eastbourne in the thirties, Queen Mary came over for an informal visit. Ivy didn't see the Queen herself, because she was put in charge of Taffy, the collie, in Charlie's pantry to make sure he didn't make a nuisance of himself. Rose's niece, Myfanwy, now Mrs Mickleson, remembers that she was staying at Brompton Square as a small girl once, and she ran and opened the door to the Queen or Princess Alice, Countess of Athlone, which she shouldn't have done. She then went and hid in a cupboard from which she saw Charlie kneel and remove the royal galoshes, which she thought very funny as the royal legs would have been on view to him. Ivy says she is certain Queen Mary never visited at Brompton Square, so possibly this episode relates to a visit by other eminent ladies, perhaps of the royal family? It could have been Princess Alice, as on 5th June 1937 she was writing to accept Mr Benson's invitation to lunch on the 10th . . . "What a lot we shall have to talk about!"

Another time Princess Alice, wearing a pink dress and a blue picture hat, came to lunch with a few other guests at Lamb House before her official function at Rye Hill. It was a beautiful day and they took a little walk in the garden afterwards; noticing Mr Benson's shoelace was undone, she bent down and tied it up for him because of his arthritis, which he thought "extremely kind of her".

Just before the second world war, Canon Fowler's daughter, Constance, asked Mr Benson whether he would take in some evacuees; when he asked how he would entertain them, Miss Fowler suggested he could play football on the lawn with them, which made them all laugh, especially considering his arthritis at that stage. Three evacuees duly came, and they stayed until there was talk of the invasion of France, and after that any evacuees, as well as children from Rye, were sent somewhere safer. The youngest was a little boy called Billy, who was six, and Ivy used to put him to bed and hear his prayers. They went to school in the daytime, and after tea they were looked after by Rose and Ivy in the kitchen until bedtime, with Billy reading them bits about the war from the evening paper.

She remembers that almost every morning when he got up Mr Benson would go downstairs and play the tune *In an English Country Garden* on the piano, which was a sort of signal that he was ready for breakfast. At Christmas they would decorate a very small Christmas tree, which was sometimes one which had survived bedded out from the previous year, and this stood on the dining room sideboard, hung with baubles, glass peacocks, red candles and tufts of artificial snow. Christmas would be celebrated with a few old friends, people such as Canon Fowler and his daughters.

Ivy also remembers Mr Benson having shingles very badly on his face, while he was writing *King Edward VII*—she thinks it was probably partly a result of the hard work the research involved. So when he was writing about Georgie's shingles, he was writing from personal experience. As Lucia was eventually admitted to see Georgie, so Radclyffe Hall called on Benson, and was heard to exclaim "You poor darling!" when she saw him.

Whereas Charlie was given copies of many of Mr Benson's books, Ivy only remembers being given one. Charlie had happened to mention to Mr Benson that Ivy's birthday fell on 21st March, the same day as his mother, Mary Benson's, and so he inscribed and gave her a copy of his novel *Secret Lives*. She also told us that he had given his final volume of autobiography some other name originally (she doesn't remember what it was), but realising it would be his last he re-named it *Final Edition*.

Ivy tells of two memories from 25 Brompton Square in the '20's or '30's: "Mr Benson had an evening appointment at the BBC to read one of his stories on the radio . . . I think he had £5 for reading it. We took Taffy up to the drawing room, and he sat on Mr Benson's chair with the earphones on. He was a little excited, and made a pleasant noise, and we were convinced he recognised 'His Master's Voice'! On another occasion we had Dame Nellie Melba to lunch, with just a few other guests. One was a Russian pianist, his name was Prince George Chavchavadze. After lunch Dame Nellie Melba sang *Home Sweet Home* accompanied by the Prince at the piano, so Mr Benson opened the drawing room door, after ringing the bell, for us three to listen. It was beautiful."

Rose Edwards, as she was then (she later married Charlie of course), knew Ivy before she came to work for Mr Benson, and recommended her for the job. Rose and Charlie were courting for years, without Mr Benson having the slightest idea apparently. Rose could get jealous, and there were quite a few arguments down in the kitchen at times, the worst being after he'd been out with another girl when he was away in Cley-Next-the-Sea, in Norfolk. On that occasion Rose was so furious that she smashed a record of *Swanee River*. Rose and Ivy used to teach themselves to dance to these gramophone records when Mr Benson and Charlie were away, covering the kitchen floor with French chalk to achieve the required slippery effect. One day Mr Benson asked Rose whether he might accompany her on her marketing in Rye High Street, because he wanted to meet all the shopkeepers they used, and Rose was very proud of this.

Ivy says, "I don't know of anyone E.F.B. didn't like, us three and Spicer included . . . When I said I wished to leave once, he said, 'No! I like you all!'"

2 Constance Warrender, and others

Constance Fowler (now Mrs Warrender, the widow of Lady Maud Warrender's son Harold) was then the unmarried daughter of Mr

Benson's closest Rye friend, Canon John Fowler, vicar of Rye from 1921–42. Canon Fowler dined at Lamb House every week or fortnight, and Constance was pleased when he went because he enjoyed himself so much and had such good food. At home the Canon would say that foods such as pastry, cream, butter and cheese disagreed with him, but he forgot all about that at Lamb House and ate the richest foods with relish. She was nervous on the few occasions when Mr Benson was to eat at their house, however, because she felt she had such an impossibly high standard to compete with. Then he would do something completely silly and make them roar with laughter, as when he arrived on the doorstep one night, very solemnly holding one arum lily before him. She remembers she and her sister, now Mrs Elaine Johnston, being very impressed at Christmas at Lamb House when the hot roast chestnuts were brought in wrapped in a napkin. But one Christmas memory which still rankles is that Mr Benson once used a ghost story which her father had told him, and it was published in the Christmas number of a magazine (probably the *Bystander*). She feels certain that Mr Benson didn't ask permission, nor make any acknowledgement, but it evidently didn't have any serious effect on their friendship.

Mr Benson's few surviving letters to his friend the canon are a delight to read, full of gleeful news, affectionate teasing and his still boyish exuberance. There are lots of references to food—Mr Benson used to tease the canon about the cheeses he was supposed to avoid ("You shall have plenty of different kinds of cheese.") and the burgundy he enjoyed at Lamb House. The canon had rather a blue nose, through poor circulation, so the joke was that he'd got it from drinking when in fact he almost never drank at home. In 1924 Mr Benson thanks him for some smoked Rye herrings which he had sent him and which he "will enjoy all the more in the knowledge that Queen Elizabeth would certainly have taken them away" from him—a reference to the fact that Rye was once supplier of herrings for the royal table. Sometimes Mr Benson would send the Fowlers peaches from the garden, which Mrs Warrender still remembers as being delicious. There are also frequent references to Rye's bitterly cold winds in his letters—he obviously felt the cold very much.

In March 1928 Canon Fowler presented Mr Benson with an appropriate surprise gift (possibly in gratitude for the Arthur Benson church window, given that year), a silver model of Drake's ship, *The Golden Hind*. The canon had applied to Benson for a picture of the ship, under some pretext or another, and had been sent a copy of his new book *Sir Francis Drake* which had a fairly small illustration. On March 8th Mr Benson wrote with evident delight to thank him for the model ship, which was apparently a complete surprise, saying: "The Golden Hind is too lovely and enchanting and I adore it . . ."

In a newsy letter of February 10th 1927, Mr Benson tells his friend proudly, "I walked to Iden and back [about 5 miles altogether] yesterday. You will see a leader no doubt about that athletic feat in the *Times* . . ." His arthritis must have given him one of its rare remissions. In the same letter he continues "I am writing the silliest book yet known, which will be called 'Paying Guests' . . . the garden-room resounds with the laughter of the author." This novel is in fact one of the few which is very nearly as good and as funny as the *Mapp & Lucia* books—it, *Mrs Ames* and *Secret Lives* are all in the same vein. In a letter of November 24th 1924, he refers to a young man—unnamed—as "but the faint shadow of a poopstick", and closes another letter with: "As I am getting foolish, sir, I will now conclewde."

It was these two friends, Canon Fowler and Mr Benson, who were sitting together one summer's day after lunch, in the Secret Garden near the doorway, when they both saw a ghost. It was a man in black, wearing hose and tossing the righthand corner of a cape over his left shoulder as he passed. It was bright sunlight through the doorway, so not conducive to the imagining of dark and shadowy apparitions, and they both jumped up and looked through into the main garden but no-one was to be seen. Canon Fowler glimpsed the figure again shortly afterwards, in the same place, and Mr Benson thought he might later have seen it one evening on the lawn near the Garden Room, though he was less certain about that.

In 1942, two years after Benson's death, Canon Fowler retired from Rye and went to Chicester to the quieter life of a canon there, and he died before the end of the war. He requested that his grave should be unmarked. He told his daughter that when Mr Benson was dying he said he could 'see' blue butterflies: perhaps he imagined himself back in Savernake Forest collecting butterflies as a boy? In *Our Family Affairs* (1920) he wrote that if, as he strongly believed, his spirit were one day to return to the places where he first came to love beauty, then one of the first it would fly to would be to the noble serenity of Savernake Forest. Fanciful perhaps, but Benson was always fascinated by other people's death-bed visions, so it is perhaps fitting that he should be credited with an appropriate one of his own.

Constance Warrender told us how her father's sermons were so original and therefore so popular that people from other parishes would phone up and try to book seats when he was preaching! He had intended to be an actor at one time, and retained his dramatic gifts. It is clear to us that Canon Fowler fully deserves a book of his own.

The Ellis family lived in Tower House, opposite Lamb House, and so were neighbours. Mrs William Ellis (Mildred) remembers Mr Benson popping in and out informally, and always found him very pleasant and not at all tactiturn or short with women. Her mother, Minnie, was made a magistrate (Rye's first lady J.P.) on the same day as Mr Benson was, in 1933, and used to say he always took great trouble even over the smallest offences, investigating all the circumstances in order to be as helpful as possible. Minnie's granddaughter Elizabeth Ellis (now Mrs Ashby and married to a local farmer), who was born in 1927, recalls that as children she and her brother George were allowed to go into the garden and play with Taffy whenever they liked. She was evacuated just before Mr Benson died in 1940, so possibly played there until she was twelve or thirteen. She says he was sweet with children, although possibly a little shy with adults, and he would tell them the names of the different flowers and give them chocolate, and they would sit and drink cups of Marmite drink together. He always had time for them, even if he was busy writing, and he was never angry with them if they made a noise.

Mrs Ashby also remembers Canon Fowler calling on them at home sometimes, and leaving his large wideawake hat in the hall. The children always used to try it on, and they were once caught in the act. The canon had a bird-like mind, she recalls, and was always jumping from one subject to another, and could be frightfully amusing. This description could apply equally to his daughter.

Mrs Margaret Wethey's parents were the Rye doctor, Dr Skinner, and his wife. They lived at Mountsfield House on Rye Hill and were friends of Mr Benson and both played bridge and dined with him. She said he wasn't tall but was a "man of presence", and she thought then that he used to "hold forth" at dinner.

She remembers the occasion of the royal garden party at their home, attended by the Athlones: it was possibly given in order to thank people who had worked for some charity, although she is not certain about this. Mr Benson's advice was asked about the arrangements and he said that the Skinners' Persian carpets would not be grand enough and that they should hire red carpet, so "miles of red carpet" came from a Dover undertaker. Mrs Skinner, having first rehearsed curtseying in the hall, presented a few selected guests to Princess Alice in the drawing room, where she and her husband were offered tea. Most of the guests had theirs outside in the garden, possibly in a marquee. Mountains of food were provided, including meat sandwiches, and a choice of China and Indian tea, but most of it still seemed to be left untouched at the end. This may not be unconnected with the fact that the royal party had lunched at Lamb House with Mr Benson beforehand.

Mrs Viola Bayley, a children's writer who lives in Rye, has one vivid memory of Mr Benson, but not perhaps one of the happiest, although she remembers that her mother, Mrs Powles, liked him and found him very helpful when she was on the Town Council. As a young girl of eighteen, Viola was visiting friends in Watchbell Street one evening when the doorbell rang, and there was a policeman on the doorstep. He asked whose the car outside was, and was somewhat disappointed when she said it was hers: he had thought it belonged to a local J.P. and leading citizen, Mr Delves, and as it was parked both without lights and "in an unlawful place" he had been hoping to catch the magistrate out, for a bit of fun. As it was, he had to go ahead and book Viola, whose sidelights now wouldn't work at all when she went out to switch them on. She duly received a summons, and was advised the fine would probably be smaller if she appeared in court in person.

What she hadn't realised was that Mr Benson, an old family friend, was to be the magistrate. It so happened that hers was the only case that morning, and being a wet day there was a good number of bored holiday-makers in the court, hoping for some sort of entertainment. So Mr Benson decided to play to the gallery, and spun it all out, asking the Town Clerk solemnly whether the accused had any previous criminal record, and whether there were any mitigating circumstances, and so on. The poor girl, by then seething with indignation and embarrassment, was in no position to appreciate this no doubt witty performance, which was eventually brought to a close with a fine of five shillings.

Her sister, Veronica Powles, remembers a rather nice little story about Mr Benson. He was giving a vote of thanks at a meeting, and he recalled an earlier occasion when he had to read someone else's vote of thanks, in their absence. He suddenly noticed a word which was completely unfamiliar to him and, trying not to panic, he hazarded a wild guess at pronunciation and read out "bee-ahno". The word was "beano"!

Dr John Aiken, son of the American poet Conrad Aiken and himself a writer, remembers that Mr Benson played chess with him when he was a little boy, and also he sometimes played the piano to him, Bach in particular. Although John was only a child, he felt certain that Mr Benson played the piano exceptionally well.

Mr William Bryan, acting for the solicitors William Dawes & Co., saw Mr Benson about his will during his last illness. He was amazed to find him in bed immaculately dressed (from the waist up, at least) in a tunic shirt with gold cufflinks and a tie, etc., rather than the expected night-wear.

Lady Ritchie, then Anne Burra, used to meet Mr Benson sometimes when she went to dinner with their mutual friend Mrs Jacomb-Hood. She says that he was always very kind and friendly to her, as a young woman, although at the time the conversation and the anecdotes didn't mean as much to her as they would later have done. Her particular interest in him was more in his skating expertise, and she admired his book on skating. She herself did English Style skating and confirms how difficult it was to get the balance right. She used to possess a little statuette of Mr Benson skating, but doesn't know who it was by or how many were produced. Her parents were friends of Mr Benson.

Miss Pigrome's father taught mathematics and science at the Rye Grammar School, and he was a good chess player, running the Rye Chess Club and sometimes playing chess with Mr Benson in the Garden Room at Lamb House. The first time he went there, Mr Benson asked him whether he minded sitting in a certain chair. He replied that he was quite comfortable, and Mr Benson then told him: "That was the chair Grebell died in—I often see him sitting in it." Apparently this was a sort of party trick with Mr Benson whenever he took anyone into the Garden Room for the first time: Sir Steven Runciman recounts exactly the same story. Benson seems to have embroidered when talking to his friends, if we are to believe his account in *Final Edition*. There he describes how a medium at a *séance* he arranged once saw a hunched figure in the chair, although apparently unaware of the story of the Grebell murder. He makes no mention of seeing the ghost in the chair himself, although he tells of his other ghostly sighting in the garden in the same book.

Rye Literary Institute in Market Road was something of a cultural centre of the town. There were separate ladies' and gentlemen's reading rooms, with journals, etc., and the men also played chess in theirs—the Rye Chess Club was based there. There was a billiards room upstairs, and *Deacon's Directory* for 1928 informs us that there was also "a wireless installation for the use of members". Miss Pigrome, having just read an E. F. Benson story (*The Witches' Ball?*) in a journal there and having been most impressed by its imaginative power, met the author in the street when she and her mother were together. She told him how much she had liked it, and he seemed very pleased. She remembers him as a perfectly pleasant elderly gentleman, rather than an awesome literary figure.

Incidentally, there was another Literary Society in Rye in those days—The Anchorites, which met at the Old Hope Anchor hotel.

Miss Josepha Aubrey Smith remembers Mr Benson coming to luncheon with her father, Admiral Sir Aubrey Clare Hugh Smith—they were acquaintances rather than close friends—and she remembers being taken to tea in the Garden Room at Lamb House. In contrast to most of the people we spoke to, Miss Aubrey Smith's impression was of someone "not at all inclined to take pains to be amiable" to her as a young person "and my memory is of a rather cross face".

Polly Hacking's daughter Betty, now Mrs Crosskill, also remembers being taken by her mother to tea at Lamb House as a young girl. She was rather bored by the conversations which were on literary and municipal matters. She says it was an age when young people were taken on these visits by their parents and were expected to sit and listen quietly. If anything, she found Mr Benson a bit distant, although he got on very well with her mother.

Mrs Gwen Bligh's father, J. H. Macdonnell, was a London solicitor who owned and developed much property in Rye, including the Mermaid which was his from the 1920's until the second world war. As the eldest of his six children, Gwen was expected to "traipse around behind him" on his visits, sometimes carrying books for him. She found this all rather boring, not surprisingly, but the compensation at Lamb House was the pleasure of being able to sit up in the window of the Garden Room, feeling very grand as she looked down on the passersby. She was a bit in awe of Mr Benson, and thought he didn't seem too fond of children. Whenever he went to dinner at the Mermaid, everyone was very anxious to get things exactly right. Sometimes he would tell Mr

Macdonnell to send Gwen along to Lamb House for some flowers for a special occasion at the Mermaid, but Rose Edwards, the cook, always squashed her. In fact she always struck Gwen as "bossy" and would tell her not to bang her heels on the skirting.

Councillor George Marsden, mayor at the time of E. F. Benson's death, paid tribute to his memory in the *Sussex Express & County Herald* of 8th March 1940, part of which reads as follows:

"The late Mr E. F. Benson introduced into the Council Chamber the flavour of a unique personality. His delicate sense of humour kept the Council in good temper, and frequently resolved into clarity and common sense an atmosphere befogged with prejudice or passion. Though he wore an air of detachment, he was far more conversant with the details of civic life and organisation than was commonly supposed. Few persons other than the recipients were aware of his many acts of kindness and charity.

It was a rare pleasure to partake of his hospitality at Lamb House. A meal which, though simple, was a work of art; bland vintages; the severest of old silver; urbane and witty conversation, embellished with reminiscences drawn from a widely varied experience; and afterwards perhaps a stroll in his lovely and beloved gardens. I liked the smaller one best, his sanctum . . .

In the busy streets of Rye, and in its quiet corners, many potent figures of its historic past still live and hold commune with those who have ears to hear. With these E. F. Benson is now numbered."

Earlier, in the *Sussex Express* of March 25th 1938, there is a report of Councillor Marsden's speech at the ceremony granting Mr Benson the Freedom of Rye. He said that since 1885 only six people had received the honorary freedom. "He has presided over the deliberations of the Council with incomparable charm" and in his capacity of chief magistrate, Mr Benson had a persuasive charm which surely convinced criminals that it was better to be good than clever.

There had been many persons who had been mayor of Rye longer than Mr Benson and in private benefactors the town had been singularly rich. Yet not all of them had been chosen as honorary freemen of the borough. "Why were we so unanimous in choosing him? I can answer in one sentence. It is because he has left upon the historic character of this community the vivid impress of his personality."

10 *Tatler* photograph of 2nd February 1910, p. 49. E. F. Benson at lunch between Wilfrid Coleridge (l.) and his father, the Hon. Gilbert Coleridge (r.) at Villars. Wilfrid has just passed his gold skating test.

11 Lamb House staff, autumn 1939, in the garden.
l. to r. Ivy Green, Rose Edwards, an evacuee, Charlie Tomlin, Crown.

12 E. F. Benson with Friends, early 1930's.
l. to r. Canon Fowler, E. F. Benson and the Hon. Eleanor Brougham, affectionately known as Baba (she had been a lady-in-waiting to Queen Victoria Eugenie of Spain and died unmarried in 1966). Taffy in foreground. In the background is the weeping ash which E. F. Benson always claimed to hate, although he never removed it. A. C. Benson had liked it. In the novels Miss Mapp had liked it, but Lucia, on gaining possession had it cut down.

13 Rye 1938 or 1939?, l. to r. Canon Fowler, E. F. Benson (L. A. Vidler behind), possibly Marian Dawes, Mrs Jacomb-Hood.

3 Sir Steven Runciman, and others

The Hon. Sir Steven Runciman, the distinguished scholar and historian and author of a number of books—his three-volume *History of the Crusades* and *Sicilian Vespers* are probably the best-known—was introduced to E. F. Benson by the Hon. Eleanor Brougham, a Brompton Square neighbour of Benson's, in the late 1920's. Sir Steven was at this time a don at Cambridge, and they came to know each other well. They would meet whenever Sir Steven was in London, and he came to stay at Lamb House twice. He last saw Mr Benson in about 1938.

"He was, I think, the best company of anyone I have known. He had himself known everyone of interest in his time . . . and had an immensely observant eye and had an unending store of anecdotes, all highly entertaining and some pretty libellous, though he was always discreet. 'Kindly' is not an adjective that leaps to the mind—though he was always extremely kind to me [then a shy young man of 26 or so]. His humour was a bit too sharp for that. But there was no basic malice in him, only a delight in the ridiculous. And in private life he *was* kind. The stories that he told in *As We Were*, entertaining as they are, were just slightly modified from the stories that he used to tell me . . .

He used to tell me of the progress of the later Lucia stories. I remember staying with him at Rye when he told me with delight of his plan, that he had just thought of, to send Lucia and Miss Mapp away to sea on the kitchen table." At the time, Sir Steven was not quite sure about its rightness, but he now feels that it is masterly and lifts the novels out of mere social comedy on to a wider horizon of fantastic and surrealist humour. He knows them really well, and says one feels with all the characters and doesn't know whose side one is on. When asked how Mr Benson would have known the minutiae of behaviour lower down the social scale, Sir Steven spoke of Mr Benson's intense interest in what was going on, both from his own keen observation and what he learned from gossip and so on. He also remembered that there had been an ordinary, comfortable sort of a lady in Rye, whose name he has forgotten—probably Mrs Jacomb-Hood—who might have taken him to places like Diva's Tea Rooms. Mr Benson acknowledged to Sir Steven that there was a lot of himself in Lucia: he told others he was Mapp. *Dodo* was already dated even when Sir Steven first read it; it had placed Benson a little outside the social pale, as he had to some extent let the side down by writing satirically of his own class. For this reason, Sir Steven's parents did not altogether approve of the friendship.

On his second Rye visit, they saw the R101 airship on a trial run, shortly before its disastrous final flight. He remembers Mr Benson referring to Radclyffe Hall and Una Troubridge, who were living in Rye, as "the girls", and his feelings towards them were perhaps a little equivocal—for instance he would say "I think you might be *amused* to go to tea with the girls." Sir Steven's impression of the garden at Lamb House was that it was perhaps rather bare, if anything, although green and trim.

When they went into the Garden Room, Mr Benson asked Sir Steven if he felt anything about any of the furniture and he replied that the chairs made him slightly uneasy. He didn't know that one of them was believed to be the chair in which Grebell had died and Mr Benson told him that he had once seen a hunched figure in that chair. He seems to have been exaggerating, as he later wrote that it was a medium who saw the ghostly figure slumped in the chair. Mr Benson also told him of another supernatural experience, when he stayed in a house that was supposed to be haunted. The hostess told him that he need not worry about the ghost as it was not hostile. As he lay in bed he heard a figure approaching, tapping its way along the wall of the corridor. He was absolutely terrified, but instantly relieved as soon as the sounds had passed his door.

Sir Steven always addressed his friend as 'Mr Benson' which would have been the "only proper mode of address", and Mr Benson called him Steven. Although Benson had friends to whom he was sincerely devoted, of all ages and both sexes, there were not actually very many young people—Sir Steven always seemed to be the youngest person at his parties. Benson much enjoyed royal connections.

Mr Benson and Lord Stanmore enjoyed an eccentric sort of competition in which they collected the appalling poems which Queen Alexandra used to put on funeral wreaths; they were either doggerel or strange and ungrammatical free verse. The rivalry was deadly serious and neither would share his transcriptions with the other. Mr Benson promised to leave this collection to Sir Steven, but he never heard any more of it. Two examples, recalled years later so possibly not word-perfect:

Sir Dighton Probyn

To dear old Dighton Probyn,
For all that he has been to us,
For all these years—forty-seven years;—

But he has gone before to Heaven,
Where he will pull us up. God bless.

Lady Feodora Gleichèn (a sculptress)

To my darling Feo Gleichen,
Who was always dear to my heart,
Whose loss I shall always miss
Nor her wonderful works of art.

This relish in bad poetry and its bathos prompted Benson to make a collection of gems from Poets Laureate, and Alfred Austin in particular (see *As We Were*) and the same sense of humour was responsible for a most delightful and hilarious scrapbook which he compiled with Philip Burne-Jones, the son of the pre-Raphaelite painter and himself an artist. For some reason, probably because he was pompous, they decided to quite privately send up Lord Desborough, a public figure of the day, and they cut his name from all newspaper reports they came across and painstakingly inserted it into other, totally incongruous news items. Even to someone knowing nothing of Lord Desborough, these are still extremely funny.

Sir Steven, being himself very tall, had the impression that Mr Benson was small in stature, and he speaks of his great courage because, although in really excruciating pain from his arthritis for much of the time, he always put on a tremendously cheerful front before other people.

When Sir Steven was due to sit next to Dame Nellie Melba at a meal, Mr Benson warned him that she would tell very coarse stories at which he should laugh heartily. She did and he did.

Benson "knew he wasn't a great writer" but would have liked to have been, and Sir Steven feels that he would have been both amazed and pleased at the existence of an appreciation society (The Tilling Society) so many years later. He doesn't think that the *Mapp & Lucia* novels made a great stir when they first came out; the thirties were a serious time and they were probably considered too trivial. However, the actor, John Wyse, tells us that the books were a cult up to and even during the second world war. See also the end of the next contribution, by Betty Askwith.

Betty Askwith's recollection of Mr Benson is not strictly a Rye one, although her mother, Lady Askwith, did take her to tea with him once in the Garden Room at Rye. Betty (who herself became a writer and did an excellent short biography of the Bensons in *Two Victorian Families*) was allowed by her mother to sit next to Mr Benson at a luncheon party at their house in Cadogan Gardens in around 1922, when she was only about thirteen. She says she had, rather precociously, just been reading his *Dodo* and told him she "didn't care much for it," which he kindly passed over, but she thinks he was genuinely pleased when she said how much she loved and admired *David Blaize*. "He told me as a great secret that another sequel was on its way [*David of Kings*, 1924] and that his mother had been entirely of my opinion and liked *David Blaize* much the best of all his books."

She remembers him as "not tall, but very erect and rather soldierly looking with thick grey-white hair and a clipped grey moustache and large luminous blue eyes."

A few months later he called at their home in Sunningdale to ask after her grandmother, Lady Georgiana Peel, who was dying. "I remember the parlourmaid saying that Lady Askwith was out but perhaps 'Miss Betty' would know, and his voice saying: 'Perhaps I could have a word with Miss Betty?' It was the highest, headiest excitement because he was so charming and treated one exactly as if one were grown up and important."

When her first book came out, she had lunch with him in Brompton Square, but doesn't retain any vivid impression of that occasion. She remembers that the *Mapp & Lucia* books were much read and talked about in society, and that Lucia was "confidently equated with Lady Colefax". Incidentally, it is some measure of the general popularity of the novels that in 1932 the *Daily Mail* Ideal Home Exhibition had a Mapp & Lucia garden, by Carters Tested Seeds.

Finally, there are memories from two ladies which are remarkable for the fact that they go back to Hugh Benson, and to Mary Benson, the mother, although they don't directly concern E. F. Benson.

Mrs Clara Carnell was born Clara May Farrow in 1883, and was the daughter of a Church of England clergyman in the West Riding of Yorkshire. So impressed was she by one of Hugh Benson's novels, *The Conventionalists,* that she asked to meet him, not realising that he was a priest, to ask his advice and to discuss the book. She found his advice so wise and helpful that she became interested in the Catholic faith, and became a Catholic herself shortly afterwards. On another occasion she and a friend went and had tea with him at Hare Street House, near Buntingford, where he lived so happily for his last years. Another time he came to tea at the boarding house in Bayswater where she was living while she studied music. They didn't meet often, but a firm friendship developed through their letters, which lasted until his early death. In 1984 Mrs Carnell still remembers and writes of this with absolute clarity.

Mrs Mylne, now in her 98th year, was born Kathleen d'Esterre Hubbard. Her husband, the Rev. Charles Mylne, was the son of 'Tan' Mylne (wrongly given as 'Tau' in some biographies), a nickname, as she was actually christened Caroline Charlotte. Tan was one of Mary Benson's close friends in the early years of her marriage, and their friendship endured—Tan had had a strong spiritual influence on Mary, and helped her find a new faith which was more instinctive and benevolent than that of her husband, the Archbishop. When Tan's son got engaged, the young couple were sent to Tremans for a long weekend in 1911 in order that Mary could 'look over' his fiancée. It was quite a frightening experience for a young girl; she had a new black velvet evening dress for the occasion, which was a great success, much to her relief. A small sittingroom upstairs next to the chapel, was put aside for their use. When they got married, Mary Benson was one of their principal wedding guests. (We owe this information to Major Boris Mylne, son of Charles and Kathleen Mylne.)

Part IV

Tilling and fellow inhabitants of Benson's Rye—with introduction

Apart from the real buffs who know the Tilling books almost by heart, the average devotee cannot always turn up a particular incident rapidly. So we have listed the contents fairly concisely, chapter by chapter. There is only one exact date given—for the cenotaph—but the other books can be dated through the seasons before and after that date.

The descriptions of the characters and the places in Tilling are scattered throughout the six *Mapp and Lucia* books, and, having gathered them together, we felt that other enthusiasts might find it interesting and useful to see them set down in one place. We found that until we did this we had only the vaguest idea what some of the

TILLING			RYE
MALLARDS	1		LAMB HOUSE
The Garden Room	1b		
Captain Puffin	2		Little Sussex House
Major Flint	3		Opposite Little Sussex House
Mallards Cottage	4		
Poppits	5		The Old Customs House
Padre	6		The Old Vicarage
HIGH STREET	7		HIGH STREET
Diva (Wasters, later Ye Olde Tea House)		a	The Mariners
The King's Arms		b	The George
Twistevant's (Greengrocer)		c	
Twemlow's (Grocer)		d	
Worthington's (Butcher)		e	
Post Box		f	
Stationer's		g	
Mr. Rice (Poulterer)		h	
Post Office		i	
WEST STREET	8		WEST STREET
Irene (Taormina)		a	No. 2
Hopkins' (Fishmonger)		b	Cobble Cottage
Fruiterer		c	The Other House
PORPOISE STREET	9		MERMAID STREET
Dentist		a	First House on the left
Wyses		b	Hartshorn House
MALLESON STREET	10		MARKET ROAD
Dr. Dobbie		a	
Woolgar & Pipstow		b	
CURFEW STREET	11		WATCHBELL STREET
Trader's Arms		a	Hope Anchor
Viewpoint Terrace		b	
Suntrap		c	Watchbell Corner
Norman Tower	12		Ypres Tower
Town Hall	13		Town Hall

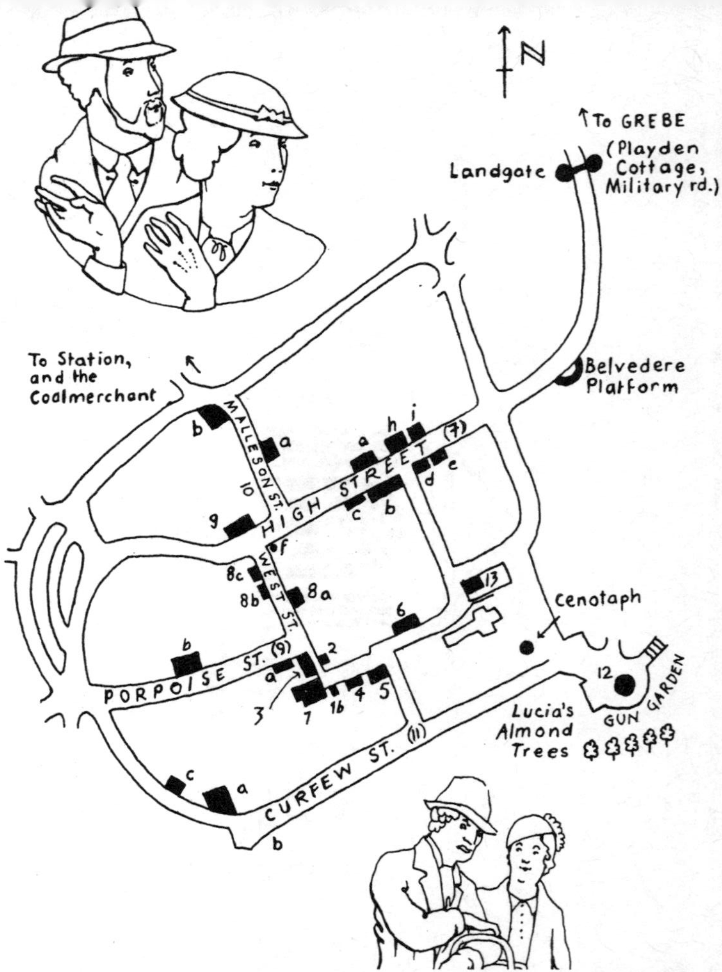

14 Map of Tilling, with the probable Rye locations of the Tilling inhabitants. Drawn by Katharine Stephen.

characters looked like, and sometimes even had a completely wrong impression—on a first reading we imagined Georgie as small, for example, when really he is tall. And it was only after assembling the information that we came across a description of a real person in *Final Edition* which exactly tallied with Algernon Wyse. Perhaps further identifications will follow.

Gathering the topographical references enabled us to work out a detailed new map relating Tilling to Rye (we are grateful for the original map Aubrey Woods compiled, which set us on the right track in the first place), and we follow this with our explanations. Some placings are unequivocally right, others are less definite, and a few are pure guesswork.

It is always intriguing to speculate who might have been the inspiration for the various fictitious Tilling characters, and we have collected together whatever has been suggested to us and our own speculations. For the situations, we have only scratched the surface, as the more one learns about Benson the more one realises that almost every fictitious event is based on his first-hand experience or that of some friend.

This section ends with a fairly lengthy chapter on the people who lived in Rye at the same time as E. F. Benson; the chapter on 'originals' leads on naturally to this, and we have tried to cover as many as possible of his neighbours and the people who were possibly acquaintances and friends. Others mentioned would have served with him on the Town Council and on committees, etc., and some would have been known to him in their professional capacities. Probably the people who lived in Rye during the last few years of Mr Benson's time have been given greater coverage than the earlier ones, simply because more is remembered about them. We have left the more enthusiastic reader to compare factual and fictitious Tilling/Rye co-habitors.

1 Order of events in the Tilling novels

Miss Mapp (July—Christmas 1929)

Chapter 1: Tilling and main characters introduced—Lucia of course does not appear at all in this book. *Chapter 2:* Alcoholic redcurrant fool served at Poppits' bridge party, and Mrs Poppit returns with MBE; Prince of Wales expected at station. *Chapter 3:* Diva decorating costume with chintz roses; Flint and Puffin arrange to write/drink together at nights; food and coal hoarding under way; Mapp sees Adam model in

Irene's studio. *Chapter 4:* Mapp upstages Diva's chintz idea and Diva retaliates; Mapp's food câche discovered. *Chapter 5:* Flint and Puffin challenge one another to a duel, but both flee. *Chapter 6:* Tilling inhabitants watch return of 'duellers' and Padre; Mr Wyse introduced. *Chapter 7:* Mapp spreads rumours that she was cause of duel; she and Diva appear in identical teagowns; Mr Wyse shows interest in Mrs Poppit. *Chapter 8:* Mapp discovers Flint/Puffin drinking secret but they see her blank 'letter' and blackmail her into silence; Mapp realises they funked duel and tells all Tilling. *Chapter 9:* Flint apologises to Mapp and accompanies her on a very public marketing spree; Puffin apologises. *Chapter 10:* Mapp and Diva appear simultaneously in identically dyed tea-gowns, then agree Diva will re-dye hers; Mr Wyse seen kissing Mrs Poppit. *Chapter 11:* Dinner at Mr Wyse's—Diva accidentally excluded until last-minute phonecall; she has no time to change so she and Mapp are identically dressed again; the Contessa arrives; Wyse/Poppit engagement. *Chapter 12:* Christmas, and death of Puffin. *Epilogue:* Mapp learns golf to prevent Flint feeling lonely; Wyse/Poppit wedding. Then follows the story of *The Male Impersonator,* a September interlude which could have taken place at any time before Lucia's arrival.

Mapp & Lucia (June 1930–April 1931)

Chapter 1: Riseholme, and Lucia is becoming restless with her long mourning; she sees Mapp's advertisement to let Mallards. *Chapter 2:* Lucia and Georgie motor to Tilling, shown over Mallards, terms agreed; they stay the night at the Trader's Arms; Diva's and Irene's dependent lets arranged. *Chapter 3:* Georgie rents Mallards Cottage; Lucia puts his mind at rest over undesirability of matrimony for them; Daisy 'persuades' Lucia to save foundering Riseholme fête by taking star part. *Chapter 4:* Lucia is installed at Mallards after triumphant fête; Cadman's and Foljambe's intended marriage announced; Lucia, irritated by Mapp's pushiness, resolves to do something about it; begins by clearing up matter of employment of Mallards gardener. *Chapter 5:* Mapp breaks Mallards doorchain; open warfare over Lucia's proposed fête; Mapp holds rival jumble sale; Mapp rejects Lucia's and Georgie's art show submissions; Mallards fête takes place and it is revealed that the hanging committee never saw the rejected pictures; Lucia magnanimously spares Mapp outright exposure. *Chapter 6:* Signs of rebellion by Tillingites over Lucia's airs; arrival of Contessa forces Lucia to feign influenza and Georgie to flee to Folkestone; he sends Italian letter which Lucia copies; succeeds in impressing Contessa; Mapp sees Lucia exercising on lawn but no-one interested. *Chapter 7:* Lucia and Georgie decide to stay on in Tilling—lobster *à la* Riseholme lunch to celebrate. *Chapter 8:* Lucia moves to Grebe, Mapp returns to Mallards; Mapp mimics Lucia's baby-talk to Georgie; Lucia's revenge is to fully expose Mapp's high-handed picture rejection, and to socially exclude her. *Chapter 9:* Lucia organises calisthenics class; Christmas. *Chapter 10:* Mapp and Lucia swept away in flood, on kitchen table. *Chapter 11:* Flint to inherit Mallards and Georgie Grebe, and both money; Georgie waits delicately before taking possession, and erects a cenotaph to both ladies after memorial service; Flint precipitously buys a car and puts his house up for sale. *Chapter 12:* April 1st and the castaways return, to see cenotaph and find crestfallen Flint in residence at Mallards; he is unceremoniously ejected; Georgie genuinely delighted at Lucia's return and she recounts her adventures to him. *Chapter 13:* Mapp tells Diva her version; Mapp and Lucia hold rival simultaneous public readings of their maritime experiences—everyone goes to Lucia's except for Mapp and Flint, who end up engaged; Mapp serves lobster *à la* Riseholme at the celebration lunch and everyone realises how she got recipe.

Lucia's Progress (January 1932—May 1933)

Chapter 1: Lucia coming up to 50 and feeling stale and restless; Georgie is incommunicado; Mapp-Flints bill and coo. *Chapter 2:* Lucia allowed to visit Georgie who has shingles and a beard; he is persuaded to stay secretly at Grebe; Lucia begins financial career, other Tillingites follow suit. *Chapter 3:* Financial speculation continues; Georgie appears in dyed Van Dyck beard. *Chapter 4:* Mapp and Lucia contest council seat—much canvassing; Irene leads noisy demo.; Mapp and Lucia tie bottom of poll. *Chapter 5:* Mapp's 'pregnancy'; she is forced to sell Lucia Mallards. *Chapter 6:* Lobster *à la* Riseholme for Lucia's house-warming lunch; Mapp trims skirt with tiger-rug strips and expected baby proves to be 'wind-egg'; gas-leak reveals remains which Lucia believes to be Roman. *Chapter 7:* Excavation rumours continue, but Lucia finds they are unfounded. *Chapter 8:* Unfortunate dinner at Wyses, with many gaffes and much awkwardness, and Flint drunk. *Chapter 9:* To cool general animosity, Lucia embarks on rôle as Tilling benefactress; flying visit of Contessa. *Chapter 10:* Dedication of renovated organ with colourful procession and garden-party—Lucia basks in the glory and publicity. *Chapter 11:* August, and house-swapping as usual; Lucia gives the town almond trees and is elected president of Cricket and Football Clubs; Mapp-Flints washed out of rented hut and are put up at Mallards, and Padre's wife follows; Lucia co-opted onto Town Council. *Chapter 12:* Lucia and Georgie decide on companionable marriage; splendid wedding; Lucia elected as next Mayor.

Trouble for Lucia (October 1933—Autumn 1934)

Chapter 1: Georgie put out by Lucia's grandiose ideas but consoled by new velvet suit; Mrs Wyse has sat on her budgerigar and now wears remains. *Chapter 2:* All Lucia's female friends put themselves forward for Mayoress, supported by husbands; Mr Wyse too appears in a new velvet suit and his wife drops budgerigar into raspberry soufflée. *Chapter 3:* Lucia asks Mapp to be Mayoress; Irene sends silly photo of Mapp to a local paper and Flint rushes off to horsewhip editor but gets tipsy and leaves whip behind; Mapp retrieves it but drops it in Diva's new tea rooms; dog quietly eats all but silver top, which Diva later finds and buries; mayoring ceremonies and banquets; Lucia unofficially opens tea rooms. *Chapter 4:* Lucia cold-shouldered when she gives up stakes in bridge; Georgie stands in new council elections but Mapp wins; Mapp has jam puffs *contretemps* with Diva. *Chapter 5:* Lucia relents over 'gambling', then card room is 'raided' by police, causing panic; Lucia and Georgie learn to cycle—incidents with tar-pot; Lucia arranges disappearance of budgerigar as Mrs Wyse seems to be growing unbalanced; confusion of Mapp's and Lucia's false teeth. *Chapter 6:* Georgie finds cap of lost whip; he and Lucia make public cycling debut—Lucia fined for dangerous driving and becomes a heroine; cycling becomes the rage. *Chapter 7:* Lucia's idea for special royal fish train rejected; she arranges a series of local talks; Mapp pockets whip cap at Mallards and has new cane fitted and Flint produces it at his talk on tiger-shooting; Lucia and Georgie have a replica made to puzzle Mapp-Flints; Irene's picture caricaturing Mapp and Flint is chosen R.A. Picture of the Year. *Chapter 8:* Lucia and Georgie go to Olga's opera, then lunch with her and Duchess of Sheffield; they visit Olga at Riseholme. *Chapter 9:* Humiliation for Lucia over visit to the duchess, and she returns to find Georgie and Olga at Mallards; Tilling ladies emulate Olga's makeup and waved hair. *Chapter 10:* Tilling art show, and pride of place to Irene's Picture of the Year plus one commissioned by Lucia; Mapp-Flint's house rented by novelist Susan Leg (Rudolph da Vinci) and Mapp and Lucia vie for her socially. *Chapter 11:* Lucia's nadir—Georgie visits Olga in France, causing gossip; council rejects Lucia's offer of her portrait; the duchess comes to Tilling and almost snubs her; rectifies matters by phoning and asking to stay night at Mallards, but no-one believes Lucia next day. *Chapter 12:* Georgie postpones his return; Lucia lets rip a tirade at all her disloyal friends and feels better; Georgie returns, and the duchess comes to stay again—this time everyone invited to dinner and all ends triumphantly for Lucia.

Working backwards from the Tilling books, we can date the first two Lucia books as follows: *Queen Lucia,* July 1926 to March 1927; *Lucia in London,* April 1928 to September or October 1928. Philip Lucas would have died in June 1929, and then a year passes before the opening of *Mapp & Lucia* in June 1930. Benson's chronology for Olga's one-year tour is contradictory, and confusion ensues if one attempts to date anything from references to it. At the beginning of *Queen Lucia,* Lucia had lived in Riseholme for ten years, since 1916.

2 Tilling topography

(To be used in conjunction with the Tilling map)

TILLING

"There is not in all England a town so blatantly picturesque as Tilling, nor one for the lover of level marsh lands, of tall reedy dykes, of enormous sunsets and rims of blue sea on the horizon, with so fortunate an environment. The hill on which it is built rises steeply from the level land, and, crowned by the great grave church, positively consists of quaint corners, rough-cast and timber cottages, and mellow Georgian fronts." (*Miss Mapp,* opening of chapter 2.)

The TILLING of the books is based closely on *Rye,* and named after the *River Tillingham.*

MALLARDS . . . "charming little panelled parlours with big windows letting in a flood of air and sunshine . . . a broad staircase with shallow treads . . . plain, well-shaped rooms . . . All looked so white and comfortable". It is first described as being Georgian, but later referred to as Queen Anne. There is a passage from MALLARDS to PORPOISE STREET. The original is *Lamb House,* now owned by the National Trust.

THE GARDEN ROOM . . . "one window shaded with the big leaves of a fig tree, through which, unseen, Miss Mapp so often peered to see whether her gardener was idling." A flight of eight steps with a canopy of wisteria leads to it. THE GARDEN . . . "a very green and well-kept lawn set in bright flower-beds; a trellis at one end separated it from a kitchen garden beyond, and round the rest ran high brick walls over which peered the roofs of other houses. In one of these walls was cut a curved archway with a della Robbia head above it". Across the lawn is the Secret Garden through an archway with a door. In the middle of its lawn is a pillar with a bust of Queen Anne. [*Note:* it would not in fact have been possible to have seen Lucia doing her calisthenics in the Secret Garden from the church tower, unless she was right in the doorway itself.] The Secret Garden is now no longer owned by Lamb House. MALLARDS is owned by Miss Mapp, then let to Lucia, then re-occupied by Miss Mapp, and finally bought by Lucia.

MALLARDS COTTAGE . . . "the sweetest little gabled cottage". It has a hall with a pretty staircase, three bedrooms and two attics. It has a tiny square of flower garden, with a patch of crazy paving surrounding a brick pillar, on top of which stands a copy of the Neapolitan Narcissus. In *Miss Mapp* it starts life as her gardener's cottage, but either this is conveniently forgotten later, or perhaps Susan Wyse has re-possessed it? Anyway, it belongs to Susan Wyse who leases it to her daughter, Isabel Poppit, who then sublets it to Georgie. It is the first cottage at the end of MALLARDS/*Lamb House* garden wall, and now has no name or number.

MAJOR FLINT'S RESIDENCE, unnamed, stands just below MALLARDS/*Lamb House,* on the same side, and is of Georgian red brick like MALLARDS. It is now a separately occupied house. Although identified as the *Lamb House Annexe,* it has no name or number up.

CAPTAIN PUFFIN'S HOUSE, also unnamed in the books, is a small, narrow house immediately opposite Major Flint's. It is now named *Little Sussex House*.

YE SMALLE HOUSE (YE OLDE HOUSE in American editions) stands "just around the corner beyond the gardener's cottage [later MALLARDS COTTAGE] and opposite the West end of the church" and has a notorious crooked chimney, often sketched and painted by aspiring artists in the novels. It is the home of the Poppits, and is now called *The Old Customs House*.

THE PADRE'S VICARAGE. There are few references and virtually no clues for this, but we have plumped for the most picturesque of the old rectories, *The Old Vicarage* right beside the church. It could equally well be what is now *number 15 East Street,* because that was the actual vicarage in Benson's time.

TAORMINA is a quite small converted coach house and is Quaint Irene's studio and cottage, in West Street, and is named after an Italian coastal resort. (Benson refers to the place Taormina in *Our Family Affairs* [1920] as occurring in the rambling conversations of Oscar Browning, an eccentric Cambridge don.) The original could well be *number 2,* which looks like a converted coach house although it isn't one.

HOPKINS THE FISHMONGER is said in the books to be three doors below the PORPOISE STREET turning in WEST STREET. *Cobble Cottage,* number 16, although a little further down is definitely meant for the original. There are twin shop-style windows, and *The Other House,* next door, can only be the FRUIT SHOP, which is described as being the next house down, with three steps up to the door. The steps are still there.

STARLING COTTAGE, in PORPOISE STREET, is one of the best houses in Tilling, an Elizabethan house with latticed windows and at least one bow window. It has an oak door with no handle but a green bronze bell-pull with a bobbin. There is a red brick garden wall. Inside there are oak beams on the ceilings and walls and an open fireplace of grey Dutch bricks. The Wyses live here. One reference gives it as 30 yards from MALLARDS COTTAGE, another as "not 100 yards". It is also variously given as 50 yards and 100 yards from MALLARDS. This shows us nothing except that the author has been careless! We place STARLING COTTAGE as *Hartshorn House,* an imposing timbered house in *Mermaid Street,* which answers to the description in most respects. It has an old open brick fireplace, and another with Delft tiles (blue on grey).

THE DENTIST is also in this street, and is described as "on the corner", but elsewhere "the pretty house just around the corner". That fits what is now *The First House,* and there really was a dentist in the next (now demolished) house along.

THE TRADER'S ARMS . . . "a pleasant hostelry nearby [to MALLARDS] with a view over the marsh . . . very comfortable indeed" is the place where Lucia and Georgie stay when they first come down from Riseholme to arrange to rent houses for themselves. It is now known as the *Hope Anchor,* and the fact that there really is a *Trader's Passage* running from it clinches the identification.

SUNTRAP is the home of the 'male impersonator' at the far end of CURFEW STREET from what is now *Church Square:* the nearby viewpoint terrace is described as commanding a good view both of the marsh and of SUNTRAP. This much we know. It could be placed where *Watchbell Corner* now is, and this is in a sheltered spot and has a sun platform on its roof. But equally it might be based on *Watchbell House* or on *number 18.* As it is described as an exceptionally substantial house, it could be that *St Anthony* was transposed to the far end of CURFEW STREET (now *Watchbell Street*). We know that *St Anthony*'s current position is wrong, since at one stage Miss Mapp is supposed to have "retraced her steps" from SUNTRAP to MALLARDS, having been diverted on her way home from the Gun-Garden. *St Anthony* would have been on her route, without any need either for a diversion or a retracing of steps.

GREBE . . . "white house that skirts the marsh, half a mile away from Tilling." There is a "nice garden sheltered from the wind" and "a dyke and a bank just across the road, keeping back high tides in the river." There is a thick hornbeam hedge, and the old cliff close behind, and the rooms face south and towards the sea. The kitchen is a separate wing, having once been a coach-house, and has double doors. There is a garage and a cottage attached. Lucia first owns it after renting MALLARDS, then she sells it to Miss Mapp when she buys MALLARDS for herself. The original for GREBE is generally believed to be *Playden Cottage* in Military Road, although we are not certain of the basis for this: it is certainly in the right direction, on the right road, and the right sort of distance away, so will do very well.

MR WOOTEN THE COALMERCHANT is at a sharp corner outside the station. One can't place it more exactly.

The great grey NORMAN TOWER, with its south-facing Gun-garden from which Miss Mapp sketches, is now the *Ypres Tower.* Mapp and Lucia come up the steps here when they return from their adventure at sea, and Lucia later has them repaired and has almond trees planted on the bare slopes below the Gun-garden.

The BELVEDERE PLATFORM gives a "delightful prospect" at the end of the High Street, and is "built on a steep slope to the east of the town". The inhabitants of Tilling congregate there to watch for the return of the duellers on the golf-links tram—this was once a real tram,

15 Garden Room photograph by Nathaniel Lloyd of Great Dixter. Date unknown. Chair on right is the one in which Grebell is believed to have died.

16 F. Yeats-Brown and E. F. Benson on the steps of the Garden Room, April 1931.

17 E. F. Benson writing in his Secret Garden, date not known. Bust is of Augustus.

18 E. F. Benson and Taffy in Lamb House garden. Early 1930's, photograph by Charlie Tomlin.

and its terminus could have been seen from there. From the same vantage-point they later see Mapp & Lucia swept away below them on the kitchen table on the flooded river whose real name is the Rother (three rivers converge in Rye—the Tilling, the Rother and the Brede). There are now two such viewpoints from *Hilder's Cliff,* and we have taken the artistic liberty of settling for the one immediately at the end of the High Street, since this was the one E. F. Benson gave to the town himself. He gave it in about 1935, so we have to decide whether he was visualising it in his novels, or whether he used the existing one (along to the left) for these incidents.

The HIGH STREET in the novels is highly populous and placings of the original businesses can sometimes only be approximated. The STATIONERS must be about where *Barclay's Bank* now is, to have been visible from the GARDEN-ROOM. WASTERS/DIVA'S TEA-ROOMS/YE OLDE TEA-HOUSE is probably where *The Mariners* now is, as we know they are directly opposite THE KING'S ARMS, which is indisputably *The George* now. However these tea rooms are also described in different places as opposite both TWISTEVANT THE GREENGROCER and TWEMLOW THE GROCER, so these shops must be quite diagonally 'opposite' really. They can reasonably be assumed to be on either side of the KING'S ARMS. TWEMLOW is also once described as being "ten yards past Diva's" (away from MALLARDS) and on the opposite side. The POST OFFICE is on the opposite side to MR WORTHINGTON THE BUTCHER, and "they walked back from the POST OFFICE to Diva's", so that gives us the correct sides of the road for these two businesses. Also, there really were a *Post Office* and the main *Butcher* and the *Grocer* on those respective sides of the High Street in Benson's day. We've placed the Tilling BUTCHER where *Ashbees* was then and still is now, and where Mr Benson's meat was bought. MR RICE THE POULTERER is next to the POST OFFICE, and probably before it coming from MALLARDS. Various other shops are fleetingly mentioned without any topographical details—*e.g.* another GROCER, called CANNICK, a second FISH SHOP "at the end of the High Street" furthest from MALLARDS; a HAIRDRESSER & COSMETICS SHOP, and a TOYSHOP; SPENCER THE PLUMBER, a TOBACCONIST and a HABERDASHERS.

MALLESON STREET is off the High Street on Diva's side. Here we have DR DOBBIE, the leading doctor, and also WOOLGAR &

PIPSTOW, the busy estate agents. This is probably what is now *Market Road*. It could alternatively be placed as the present *Conduit Hill*, but there would probably have been some reference to its cobbles and its steepness for pedestrians if that had been intended. Incidentally, in Captain Puffin's day the doctor was a Dr Brace.

Rye is also used as a setting for other E. F. Benson novels, notably: *The Oakleyites*, *Pharisees and Publicans*, *Robin Linnet*, and *Mrs Ames* where Riseborough is loosely based on Rye and the Evans's house is clearly meant to be Lamb House.

RISEHOLME (*Broadway*, in the Cotswolds) to TILLING is at first supposed to take from early morning to mid-afternoon by car; by the final book Lucia is managing the drive in only three hours. So there are no real clues as to the location of RISEHOLME to be found here.

3 Tilling Residents

MISS ELIZABETH MAPP (later MRS MAPP-FLINT): "might have been forty, and she had taken advantage of this opportunity by being just a year or two older". Her face was of a high vivid colour, and corrugated by chronic rage and curiosity. She was tall and portly, with plump hands, and fat white feet, a broad benignant face and dimpled, well-nourished cheeks, rather bulgy eyes and an expansive mouth. She had a cooing, velvety voice. She was superficially a rollicking good-natured figure of a woman, with a genial mode of address, mobile features, and a practically perpetual smile when observed. She markedly drew back her lips in speaking, being in no way ashamed of her long white teeth—which of course turn out to be false. "Rather like a hyena—not hungry now but might be." She weighed 11½ stone, and by *Lucia's Progress* was still only 43 whereas Lucia had jumped to 50 by then. Her prototype was Aunt Elizabeth (Grimson) in *The Climber*, published 1908. Miss Mapp's maid is Withers.

MRS EMMELINE LUCAS (LUCIA, later PILLSON): was 40 to begin with, but looked less, being unlined apart from a droop of skin at the corners of her mouth—artistic licence causes her age to leap to 50 in six years. She had sharp, dark beady eyes "like buttons covered with shiny American cloth". Her face was thin, oval and colourless, with, on each side of her forehead, hard, neat undulations of black hair which concealed the tips of her ears. She later has it shingled. She was "all cold alabaster without and burning with volcanic passion within" with "hands such as a sculptor dreams of but seldom sees", as a local reporter wrote, and had very pretty feet. She was the widow of the solid and well-furnished Philip or Peppino (who became Pepino) Lucas, who had acquired a fortune at the bar. Grosvenor was her maid.

GEORGIE PILLSON: was 45 at the beginning, in *Queen Lucia,* and "not an obtrusively masculine sort of person" who dressed flamboyantly. He was quite tall and nimble, with small feet, and was boyish, kind and fastidious. He was thin on top, with dyed hair and later a toupée. His face was round and pink, his eyes were blue, and he had hardly any eyebrows. He had a short nose and very red lips, with a short firm moustache which turned up at the ends, and later a dyed van Dyck beard served to hide his plump second chin, and his slightly receding first chin. His indispensable maid was Foljambe.

GODIVA PLAISTOW (DIVA): her squat rotundity of figure suited her regular, bobbing, Dutch-doll gait "like a thrush scudding over the lawn". Her speech was telegraphic, her hands were plump, and later on she had her hair in a fashionable crop. She was a widow. Her surname might have been inspired by a Chelsea landscape and flower painter of that period, called J. H. Plaistowe. Diva had an Irish terrier called Paddy and a maid called Janet.

Quaint IRENE COLES: was described as a post-impressionist artist, a suffragette, a socialist and a Germanophile. She was 25 by the final book, had a handsome boyish face, close-clipped hair, a humorous tongue and the gift of mimicry. She smoked (sometimes a pipe) and spat, and wore coloured woollen stockings with knickerbockers, or shorts and a scarlet fisherman's sweater. At other times she wore an old wideawake hat, a high-collared shirt with a stock, and a capacious jacket. Her gigantic, guardsman-like maid was Lucy.

MAJOR BENJY FLINT: He was 56, a big man though not as tall as Georgie. Given to manly guffaws, with a stiff left arm in damp weather implying he'd seen service in India, as did his use of expressions like tiffin and *qui-hi.* He was gallant and pompous to "the fairies", and intolerant of anyone who believed in ghosts, microbes or vegetarianism. He was supposed to be working on his diaries, and had a servant called Mrs Dominic.

CAPTAIN RICHARD PUFFIN: at 50 was a dried up little man, lame and short and meagre. He had a jerky, inattentive manner and a high-pitched voice, with occasional peals of falsetto laughter. He sometimes sported a panama hat. His nocturnal labours were supposed to be devoted to a history of Tilling. His servant was Mrs Gashly.

ISABEL POPPIT: had a Roman nose and a high prancing tread, and spoke in "horrid wheedling tones". She later rode a motorbike and became very brown from nude sunbathing, and her hair went all wiry. Mrs McDowall, mother of Benson's beneficiary, was also an early naturist, and Benson himself was an ardent sun-worshipper.

SUSAN POPPIT (later WYSE) MBE: was a flashy and condescending climber. She had an ample bosom and wore large fur coats. She had a fat face and a small head, and later had her grey hair waved so that it "resembled corrugated tin roofing". She occasionally wore glasses. She had a butler called Boon.

ALGERNON WYSE: a small man with a monocle, he was cleanshaven with abundant grey hair brushed back from his forehead and the face of "an actor who has seen his best days but given command performances at Windsor". He was respected and dignified. He might wear a brown velveteen coat, Byronic collar, tie with cameo ring, brown knickerbockers and stockings, and neat golfing shoes with maybe a malacca cane and panama hat. His teeth were not very good. There was an actor of the day called John Wyse, so this might have given rise to the use of a similar name for an actor-like character? Algernon Wyse's butler was Figgis.

MR BARTLETT (the Padre): interspersed archaisms with Highland expressions, and had a face which was "knobby like a chest-of-drawers". He came from Birmingham.

MRS BARTLETT (Evie): was mouselike, with a low, quick voice as though afraid of being overheard. She squealed when she was excited, and had a gliding mouselike walk and "podgy little paws". Small and thin, with a face which was sharp though timid.

SUSAN LEG (pseudonym RUDOLPH da VINCI) : comes in at the end of the Tilling books and was the heroine of E. F. Benson's *Secret Lives*, a wealthy female novelist who was a snob, without any sense of humour. She was fat, round and red, as was her face, and she looked not unlike Diva. She, like so many of the others, had podgy hands. A rude and self-satisfied woman.

AMELIA, the CONTESSA FARAGLIONE ('FARADIDDLEONY') was full of lively exuberance, and had a great sense of humour. *Faraglione* means 'rock' in Italian, and Amelia was certainly Lucia's 'rock', or danger. She was tall and lean and wore a monocle which she would drop into her food and suck clean. She smoked quantities of cigarettes, was fond of sweet coffee, sometimes winked, and wore a number of rings. She talked very fast in a shrill voice, and had a hoarse laugh. She was outspoken, flirtatious and generally enjoyed shocking the Tilling inhabitants, and then charming them. Although not strictly a Tilling resident herself, her brother Algernon Wyse's constant references to her have made the Contessa very much a presence in the town even before her long-awaited visits. Her husband was Cecco.

4 Some Origins for Tilling Characters and Situations

E. F. Benson maintained that none of his characters were based on the inhabitants of Rye, but inevitably when the *Mapp and Lucia* books came out some of the Rye people began recognising themselves and each other. Doubtless some of their characteristics and habits had been used, but the most direct inspiration seems to have been taken from people outside Rye whom Benson had known previously. It is not so strange that eccentricities repeat themselves—after all one can see Tilling equivalents in the streets of Rye today, and even the same situations recur. While we were working on this book, we treated ourselves to a bar snack lunch at the Hope Anchor (Tilling's Trader's Arms), and just before we left an elderly man and woman came in. We listened in growing disbelief as the Lucia/Georgie situation unfolded once again, with the difference that in the 1980's it was the lady who was trying to sort things out, instead of waiting delicately outside while 'Georgie' arranged it. She said that they had booked single rooms by phone, but the receptionist had apparently misunderstood and booked them into a double room. The hotel could offer them adjoining rooms in a family suite, or single rooms without bathrooms, but these alternatives were quite unacceptable to her because they were unmarried—just here on business—and anyway she hadn't even brought her dressing gown. And so it went on, the man feebly protesting that surely it was better to stay there than to wander around the other hotels in the rain, the woman indignantly determined not to stay.

We know that the sight of the shoppers hurrying about with their marketing baskets and stopping to gossip gave Benson the idea for the setting for *Miss Mapp*. We know that a great deal of house-letting went on in Rye in the summer months. We learn that Radclyffe Hall was greatly excited when she was having extensive alterations done to her house, The Black Boy, in the High Street in 1930, to find a number of ancient objects emerging from the excavations. The same thing happens to Lucia in *Lucia's Progress,* published in 1935. In 1920 Benson was awarded an MBE, and in 1922 Mrs Poppit has one in *Miss Mapp.*

We know that ghosts and the supernatural, mediums, and table-tapping held a strong fascination for Benson—he arranged for a number of *séances* to be held at various times, more than were strictly necessary just for background material. He seems to have had a certain belief in at least the possibility of the power of the medium, while recognising that many were frauds. His mother left him a mysterious package, and he took it to a number of different mediums and asked them to find out by spiritual means what it contained: all the answers were different. Radclyffe Hall and Una Troubridge were also very involved in psychical matters. In the same spirit he tried every kind of treatment for his arthritis, from cranky diets to Christian Science. He was able to laugh at himself, and at Daisy Quantock for her fervent belief in whatever cure she was currently involved in. And, like Georgie, he once suffered shingles on his face. We know he and his Rye acquaintances played bridge and golf, had dinner parties and garden parties, sketched and played the piano and held amateur art exhibitions. A painting was even hung upside-down at least once, Constance Warrender remembers, and Benson really was involved in an amusing little incident with a Rye budgerigar when he first came to the town. There really was a 'Royce' at the corner of Mermaid Street—it belonged to Mr Lloyd at The First House. We know there was an enormous number of retired majors and colonels in Rye, some of whom had served in India. And we know that Benson tended to have colourful, larger than life friends who were often considered slightly freakish for the way they followed strange fads or trends. For instance there was Dr Edward Lyttelton, who was headmaster of Eton and had a house in Norfolk and with whom Benson played golf. He was a vegetarian. Another vegetarian and health fanatic and also a follower of pelmanism, or memory-training, was Benson's long-standing friend, Eustace Miles. Yeats-Brown was obviously responsible for a certain amount of inspiration: he would pause in the writing of *Bengal Lancer* to refresh himself with breathing exercises and yoga on the lawn in the Secret Garden, and in that same autobiography he says of his time in the army in India "I had only to shout *Quai-Hai* to summon a slave." Apparently Major Benjy had a certain amount in common with Major Reeves, Secretary of the Golf Club, and with a Colonel John Watt Reid who lived at 29 Watchbell Street and was very military in his appearance and conversation. And there was an eccentric known as the 'Mad Major' who went about the streets of Rye in riding breeches and boots and leather leggings, carrying a riding crop and muttering to himself. In fact different people remember at least three quite distinct people who were known as the 'Mad Major', so the streets of Rye seem to have been positively teeming with crazed military figures! Colonel Chase, in E. F. Benson's *Paying Guests* (1929), is very like Major Benjy. Captain Bendall of the Oak House Tea Rooms may have inspired Captain Puffin.

Georgie seems to have been based on Howard Oliver Sturgis, a close friend of A. C. Benson, and the author of *Belchamber*. He did embroidery and his general description fits quite well. The *Freaks of Mayfair* (1916) by E. F. Benson gives us a preview of Georgie, although treated less affectionately at that stage, and his *Paul* (1906) has Theodore Beckwith, a mincing little man who dresses exquisitely and does embroidery. But there he is the odious villain. Interestingly, Benson seems to have grown more tolerant of Georgie types as time went on, for he tells us in *Our Family Affairs* (1920) that when he was at school he had no liking for the kind of effeminate boy who minced along with elegant gestures and flutterings. Rye people such as the Burras and the Powleses were convinced that Georgie was meant to be a portrait of Tom Hichens, who lived at Rother View in Military Road (near to Playden Cottage, the Grebe of the novels) and dressed elegantly, painted and played the piano. In fact he tended to start playing as soon as he saw someone coming up his path, in true Tilling fashion. He was a very affable man, and he died very suddenly of a heart attack in the Turkish bath one day, an end which might well have been invented by Benson.

Olga Bracely's name may have been inspired by Olga, Queen of the Hellenes, to whom Benson dedicated *The Vintage,* an early book. He used the name Princess Olga in *The Climber,* 1908, and later again in *Travail of Gold* in 1933. His friend, Yeats-Brown, married an Olga, but not until 1938. The names Daisy and Poppy also occur again in *Travail of Gold.* He certainly asked Dame Nellie Melba's advice about the habits of prima donnas, and she later said he "got it all wrong" according to the late Beverley Nichols, in a letter to us of June 1983. She said to him: "If I had practised scales like that, I should have had no voice left after five years."

We can now be fairly certain that Riseholme is based on Broadway in the Cotswolds—both Charlie Tomlin and Sir Steven Runciman were definite about this. It would have been known to E. F. Benson from visits he paid there to Mary Anderson, the American-born actress he had worshipped from afar when he was a Cambridge student. Perhaps he even felt for her something of Georgie's feelings towards Olga—a quite passionate love and admiration, as long as he wasn't expected to do anything about it? Riseholme's paper was the *Worcestershire Herald,* which fits. Tilling's local paper is the *Hastings Chronicle,* but in *Trouble for Lucia* it suddenly and misleadingly becomes the *Hampshire Argus,* probably due to re-use of incidents from Benson's existing short stories.

Benson knew several of the eccentric, mannish women of the day: there was Radclyffe Hall, who smoked black cigarettes and lived with Una Troubridge in Rye (they lived in at least three different houses there over the years). And then there was the exuberant Dame Ethel Smyth, who had originally been the friend of his sister, Nellie, and who still came to dinner with him; they also went together to take the waters at Droitwich Spa, and came back pining "for meringues and other good things forbidden there". Mrs Aubrey le Blond, in *Day In, Day Out* (1928), writes of a then recent dinner party given by Benson in Brompton Square, when Ethel Smyth was one of the guests and she was full of recollections of the brilliant conversation of the old days at the Bensons', "when five members of that family often kept a display of intellectual fireworks going for hours without a break". After this meal Benson and Ethel Smyth went through a concert she was to conduct next evening at Queen's Hall, taking the instruments on the piano in very lively manner, and Mrs le Blond writes of his versatility and the magic he drew from his little baby grand. Obviously Benson had such women as Radclyffe Hall and Ethel Smyth in mind when he invented Quaint Irene.

Algernon Wyse's description tallies exactly with that of H. E. Luxmoore in *Final Edition:* both had cleanshaven, handsome faces like those of great actors slightly past their prime; both wore knickerbockers and stockings and had neat feet; both wore brown velvet jackets, and sometimes low Byronic collars; and both were vain and dignified and expected to be treated with deference. Luxmoore was a friend and old Eton colleague of Arthur Benson.

Lucia was widely believed when the novels came out to have been based on Lady Sybil Colefax—both Betty Askwith and Harold Acton remember this was confidently held to be the case. But it seems far likelier that she was inspired by Marie Corelli. As Brian Masters says in his biography of Corelli, *Now Barabbas was a Rotter,* Benson knew her and often told amusing stories about the howlers she made and he also collected a whole boxful of information and anecdotes about her. She also used French and Italian liberally "untroubled by insufficient knowledge of either" and wrote notes in baby-talk to Arthur Severn: "When is 'oo tumin? . . . Is 'oo not velly welly? Is 'oo angry-pangry? Me misses 'oo." Corelli also lived in Stratford-on-Avon and Riseholme is obviously meant to be fairly near there in the novels. Lucia started life as Amy Bondham, heroine of three or more of his short stories, at least one of which was published in a 1924 *Tatler*. Some of Amy's exploits were identical to Lucia's, such as seeking a *cachet* 'lover'. Benson may have got the name Lucia from his time in Capri, when there was a statuesque barmaid called Donna Lucia at Morgano's Café. However, he had already used the name in 1908 for the heartless heroine of *The Climber.* In Rye it was thought that Lucia might owe something to Mrs Dacre Vincent (Margaret), who played the piano beautifully and clearly enjoyed her position as leader of the musical life of Rye.

5 Fellow inhabitants of Benson's Rye

(See also the previous chapter)

Bearing in mind that there would have been quite a bit of coming and going in the twenty-odd years that Mr Benson was in Rye, these are a few of the people who spent at least some of that time in Rye. They include neighbours and acquaintances, and many of the shops would have been used by Rose Edwards, the cook, and would have been known to Mr Benson. At this stage confusion can begin to set in if one isn't careful, and one can find oneself thinking that Rye's Mrs Jacomb-Hood couldn't have lived at The Other House because the Tilling fruiterer had his shop there, and how daring of Nurse Crawley to live with Captain Puffin in Little Sussex House!

In St Anthony in Church Square, there lived the Lloyds Bank manager, Mr H. Snow Ellis. In the Old Customs House was a Miss Queenie Bushby, a lady well-known for her good works. John Bushby, a magistrate and apparently no relation, lived in the Old Vicarage near the Church. Mr H. H. Wallis, headmaster of the Grammar School, lived in Lamb Cottage, the first cottage at the end of Lamb House garden wall and now unnamed. By 1940 a popular lady called Mrs Harry Sykes was living there. Most of the other cottages running along opposite Lamb Cottage were quite humble dwellings in those days. Peter Temple lived for many years in what is now Temple House although we don't know what year he came. He didn't mind the destruction of the Garden Room as he then got a better view of Lamb House garden. In Little Sussex House there was the efficient and well-liked Nurse Kate Crawley, and the Donovans lived next-door in Norman House. Mr Donovan had lived in Canada for many years and had a slight Canadian accent, and was said to be very pleasant. The Ellis family was in Tower House (see Mrs Ashby's separate account); they were builders and much involved in Rye's public life—aldermen, a Liberal parliamentary candidate, councillors, mayor, magistrates, etc. George and Minnie Ellis had ten children. Mr Marsden, another Rye mayor, later lived in Tower House. The next house down from Lamb House, now without name or number, used to be called The Dower House and was attached to Lamb House—Charlie Tomlin had his pantry there and his bedroom upstairs above. There was a connecting door between this annexe and Lamb House. Charlie, Rose and Ivy usually used the Dower House front door as their entrance, and its staircase as a back stairs. It is still known as Lamb House Annexe although separately occupied.

A Miss Kingsland, very old and infirm, lived at number 1 West Street with her brother, who had a secondhand shop in the cottage opposite; George Fletcher the carpenter, his wife and his son Percy at number 2; Fanny Luck at number 4; Mrs Lambert at number 5 and Mrs Rose Mawle and her son had a guest house at number 6; Mr Batcheler, who worked as a plumber for the council, was at number 7 with his wife and four children. Other Batchelers were at 5 Church Square. John Fannon was at number 8, people called Chilton at number 9, and the Mason family had Thomas House as a weekend house. Mr Mason produced Honeydew tobacco for export, and his wife was a member of the Lyceum Poetry Society and would hold poetry *soirées* in her house. There were six children. Eric, the second son, sketched; after gruelling experiences in the first world war, he married a lovely young woman and bought a farm at Iden, and was there with his family for fifty years. His widow still lives in Rye in 1984 and remembers Benson's day as a "very social time" with a number of literary and artistic people around. She thinks that Rye people enjoyed the *Mapp and Lucia* books when they first came out. At number 12 lived the slightly lame Richard Lawless Crooke—one imagines Benson the magistrate enjoying that name—and his wife, a charming couple. Albert Deason was at 13; he owned a popular off-licence, now a little shop, on the corner of Mermaid Street, and his daughter, who became Mrs Martin, ran it. Old Mrs Katharine Moneypenny lived alone at number 16. Number 17, until recently called Santa Maria, was for a while owned by Radclyffe Hall and Una Troubridge. They didn't live there but converted it and let it furnished. Mildred Ellis remembers that at one time Maypole tea and fresh butter were sold there, although it was a private house without a shop window. By 1940, a Miss D. Ramsay lived there, and John K. Beasley was at number 18. He had been a colonial administrator, or something similar, and had two daughters.

The Other House, in Watchbell Street, was a dairy. Then the Jacomb-Hoods lived there. George Percy Jacomb-Hood was an artist, influenced by the pre-Raphaelites in his early days, and an old friend of Mr Benson. He was artist correspondent for the *Graphic,* and was sent abroad to cover many royal tours; he was also sent by the *Graphic* to Greece in 1896 with E. F. Benson to gather material for the illustrations to Benson's novel *The Vintage,* which was to be serialised in that paper—he wrote of this later as "one of my most enjoyable missions . . . one of the pleasantest experiences of my life" in his autobiography *With Brush and Pencil* (1925). He died in 1929, and his wife Reta (*née* Henriette de Hochepied Larpent, one of at least five daughters of the 8th Baron de Hochepied) continued to live in The Other House, while also retaining a London house in Tite Street. She dressed well—Benson called her the most decorative lady in Rye—and she had pekinese dogs on which she, and one of her unmarried sisters who came to live with her, doted. This sister was possibly Bee, who played the violin, or Katy, who was also musical—she doesn't seem to have made a very strong impression on anyone now still living in Rye. Another sister, Sybil, married the composer Philip Napier Miles, and they lived in Bristol but often rented houses in Rye for holidays; we know they stayed at least once each at Durrant House (now a hotel), and at Norman House in West Street. Reta Jacomb-Hood became Mr Benson's mayoress from 1934–7, and is said to have been a kindly lady.

The First House, on the corner of Mermaid Street, was the weekend house of the wealthy Mr Lloyd, nicknamed 'Poppy' for some reason.

His chauffeur was known as 'Rolly' because the car was a Rolls Royce. Next door there was Mr Bowen the dentist, until about 1934. He had a good reputation as a dentist, and Mr Benson wrote reassuringly to Canon Fowler in 1935 that "Bowen is not at all disposed to extract unless there is real need for it." His house, called The Second House, was later bombed and destroyed, almost certainly in the same bombing raid which demolished the Lamb House Garden Room. Along in Hartshorn House (The Old Hospital) lived a wealthy bachelor, Humphrey Ellis, who played golf with Mr Benson sometimes. He is thought to have played golf for Cambridge. He bought the Old School opposite and gave it as a boys' club, which it has long remained. Conrad Aiken, the American poet, lived with his family at Jeakes House. His son, John, has returned to live in Rye, and his daughters Joan and Jane live in the area—all three are writers. The Old Mermaid was at one time owned by Mrs Aldington, mother of the writer Richard Aldington. The house known as The House Opposite was one of several to be developed by Mr J. H. Macdonell, and he added the beams, etc. He also owned—and altered—The Old Mermaid after Mrs Aldington. Edgar Stonham, a cornmerchant down in the Strand in Rye, was at number 4.

The Oak House Tea Rooms (now Oak Corner) was on the corner of Trader's Passage and Mermaid Street. It was run by Captain Geoffrey Bendall throughout the 1920's and until 1932, and he had a partner and friend called Charlie Green—they are said to have made an "odd couple". Then Captain Claud Moreton (who was fond of a drop of Scotch) and his wife took it over. Fletcher's House, Ye Olde Tucke Shoppe, and Simon the Pieman and the Peacock Tea Rooms in Lion Street were also all tea rooms. The Old Hope Anchor was owned by William Best, a keen cricketer, until it was bought and renovated by Miss Constance Bellhouse in the mid-1920's: she was on the Town Council when Mr Benson was mayor and she was the founder of The Anchorites Literary Society in Rye. In Watchbell Street we find Percival Swan at White House, now Swan's House (and pink), which was previously owned by a Mr Greave. Lady Tupper lived at number 24. A Mr Tayleur gave what are now called Studio One and Studio Two as a boys' club before that was moved to Mermaid Street.

At the end of the Church Square side which becomes Watchbell Street, Leopold Amon Vidler lived in Friars of the Sack, then called Stone House. He was mayor in 1927 and 1928, and in 1949 he was to become a Freeman of Rye. He wrote a history of Rye, and he and Mr Benson served on a number of committees together, such as the Chess Club, and Rye Museum which Vidler founded and of which he was curator. His son, Dr Alec Vidler, who was born in that house and returned to live there in his later years, has very kindly given us access to seventeen letters written by Mr Benson to Leopold Vidler between April 1929 and March 1938. Most are short notes concerning local matters, such as arrangements for showing mayoral parties, from Hastings and other towns, around Rye and Lamb House, and requests and acknowledgements for the loan of local books and pamphlets. Some refer to acquisitions for Rye Museum, including correspondence in 1935–6 about the possible purchase of an old map of Rye (Symondson's map) in which Mr Benson shows astuteness. He emphasises that Zaehnsdorf (from the firm selling the map), having arranged to come to Rye, "mustn't take it that a sale is being negotiated in any way at all." Later he mildly questions a claim that the firm had been offered £75 from America for the map, and finally writes rather coldly "I really only wanted to point out this morning that your arrangement with [Zaehnsdorf] was made independently of the Committee, who are therefore in no way responsible." A letter of March 5th 1936 refers tantalisingly to "a very unpleasant state of things [which] was disclosed at the Chess Committee yesterday." Until June 1936, Mr Benson closes his letters with "Yours very truly"; this then gives way to "Sincerely yours" for about eighteen months, but reverts to the more formal ending in the final two letters. Perhaps some further little coldness, or perhaps merely absent-mindedness, but it is clear that these two men were colleagues rather than close friends.

Mrs Warrender remembers some of the Rye inhabitants of these years. There was Nurse Benge, whom Canon Fowler used to refer to as his curate, because she told him all the parish news and gossip. She wore old-fashioned clothes and a bonnet which tied under her chin. There was Mr Franks, the verger (and brother of the Miss Franks who features in Charlie Tomlin's account), who was "frightfully tidy" and used to lay out the canon's vestments immaculately; the canon would then put them on any old how. Mr Franks also had the habit of coming down to tea before anyone else, so that he could get the cream off the top of the milk. There was one curate who used to take his baby everywhere with him, on parish visits, *etc.*, and this infuriated Canon Fowler, who was none too fond of children. In Cannon House lived Masters, the

Watch and Clockmaker. Mr Bowen the dentist moved to a house in East Street called Chequer in about 1934 (previously lived in by the Kingdons); when the canon had toothache, Mr Benson wrote sympathising with his "tusk trouble". The Stormonts, both artists, lived in Ockman Lane off East Street, and they left their house as an art gallery for the town. Polly Hacking, of Cadborough Farm, was an intelligent and well-read councillor and a keen gardener whose son, John, later became mayor. William Bryan remembers Major Hacking, Polly's husband, refusing to take shelter during bombing raids on Rye. So he was killed in bed one night, while Polly survived down in the cellar. Mr Bryan was among the helpers who pulled her out from the rubble, and they broke her arm doing it, but she was otherwise unhurt. Then there was Mrs Rose d'Almeida Cory whose husband had been Scout Captain of 1st Rye Captain Cory's Own Group. When he died, she took over (she was also 'cubmaster') and became the second Captain Cory and was called "Sir" by the scouts. When she felt chilly in her scout uniform she used to augment it with her feather boa. She lived in Watchbell House, Watchbell Street. And in Ockman House in East Street, Captain Dacre Vincent (known to Mrs Warrender as 'Uncle Dacre', although no relation) lived for a while. He had a brusque manner but was "a dear" when one got to know him. He was at one time Secretary of Rye Golf Club, and his wife Margaret led the musical circle in Rye and was a very kind person. They moved to Curlew in Military Road in the mid-twenties, and at one time they lived in Watchbell Street. Captain Edwin Dawes, the lawyer and Town Clerk, who was "frightfully untidy" also had an abrupt manner, but was kind and generous underneath. He lived at Spains, Rye Hill, not far from Dr Skinner and his family ("he was the grand doctor", Mrs Mason recalls) who were at Mountsfield House, where his daughter Mrs Wethey still lives. Also in that area were Lady Maud Warrender, at Leasam, and the Burras (including the artist son, Edward Burra) at a house called Springfield in Playden, just outside Rye. A great beauty, called Mrs Monkhouse, married Dick Burra on his deathbed.

The vicar, Canon John Fowler, lived at number 15 East Street. His wife, an invalid, wasn't well enough to be cared for at home, and he lived with his two daughters, Elaine and Constance, until Elaine left home and went to London. Constance stayed and kept house for her father and only married after he retired from being vicar of Rye. Playden Cottage, on the Military Road, was owned by Joseph Adams, the printer and one-time mayor, and in the late '30's he sold it to a Captain Ravenhill. The headmasters at Rye Grammar School in Mr Benson's time were first J. Molyneux Jenkins, who also served as mayor and was Mr Benson's Deputy Mayor, then H. H. Wallis (who lived next door to Lamb House in Lamb Cottage) and finally A. R. Jacobs. The Police Station was in Church Square, and the solicitors, William Dawes & Co., were in Watchbell Street. Major Reeves, of Oaklands in Udimore Road, was Secretary of the Golf Club for about ten years, until his death in 1937, and he used to play golf with Mr Benson: his daughter Ann married John Hacking, the son of Major and Polly Hacking. Dr Harratt, adored by everyone ("a dream", as Mrs Mason remembers him) lived in the Mint with his family. Dr Skinner's partner, Dr Button, treated Arthur Benson in the early 1920's, and they practised at the Hilder's Cliff end of the High Street, in what is still a doctors' surgery.

In Lion Street there was a small Greengrocer called Apps (still there in 1984), where fruit and vegetables were bought for Lamb House, as well as several lots of tea rooms. Opposite the Town Hall was Hide Brothers' Milliners and Ladies Outfitters, next to A. P. Hubbard the Baker, which became Ye Olde Tuck(e) Shoppe.

At the end of the High Street near Hilder's Cliff there was a tailor, a milliner called Truelove, and a gentlemen's outfitters, and in a house called The Black Boy lived Radclyffe Hall and Una Troubridge in the early 1930's. However they also lived at various times at a house at the end of Hucksteps Row and at a house opposite the little Catholic Church, at 8 Watchbell Street. What is now Roberts' was also a Wineshop then. The Old Apothecary on the corner of East Street was Plomley and Waters, a chemist, and Horrell's the Chemist hasn't changed its function. The little sweet shop next to the Old Grammar School was C. J. Clark the Barber, and what is now the Mariners was combined with number 16 as a Milliners and Ladies' Outfitters. The Post Office was where Liptons now is and number 94 was a haberdasher called Coates. The postmaster was Frederick Orford; he was a young Councillor in his early 30's when Mr Benson was mayor, and he remembers that although his youth made him unpopular with most of his fellow-councillors, Mr Benson was always kind and courteous, and never tried to put him down in any way. At number 93 was Collins the Greengrocer, and Jarrett ran a high-class Grocery shop where Millers now is. There was the International Tea Stores at Number 87, and

Richard Milsom the Ironmonger where Rye Bookshop now stands. What is now Martello Bookshop was Deacons until 1929 and then Gouldens, and books and stationery were sold there. Mr Deacon lived where Boots now is, and Admiral Anstruther lived at Holloway House. 95 was a Hairdresser, and Councillor Harry Schofield had a Grocery store at number 97. Another councillor, Walter Stocks, was an Ironmonger where John Dennis now is. Number 91 was a Boot and Shoe Factor. Ashbees the Butcher was Ashbees the Butcher, and Dewhursts at number 90 was in those days also a Butcher. At number 89 there was Long's the Baker, and they then had a Tea Room next door as well, where a Building Society now stands. The High Street was once called Longer Street (well before Benson's time) and so the house where Barclay's Bank now stands was called Longer House; Colonel Irvine lived there.

The study of the correspondence between real pre-war Rye and fictional Tilling is fascinating and endless. We have attempted here to gather together many fragments of information in people's memories and to record them before they were lost. Those who enjoy the *Mapp and Lucia* novels are usually passionate in their devotion and interest, and we hope this material will help to increase their enjoyment.

19 E. F. Benson, studio portrait

20 Members of Rye Borough Council with E. F. Benson, when he was made Freeman of the Borough and presented with a silver model of the *Mary Rose*. March 1938, outside Rye Town Hall.

Identification—Picture 20

1. Fred Smith, Town Sergeant 2. Canon John Fowler 3. Capt. Edwin Dawes 4. E. F. Benson 5. Councillor Marsden, Mayor 6. Jo Cooper, Deputy Mayor 7. Donald Jones 8. Mr Clark(?) 9. Police Inspector Wicken 10. J. Molyneux Jenkins (retired Headmaster) 11. Edward Curd 12. Charles A. Gafford 13. R. J. Neeves 14. Charlie Tomlin 15. Mrs E.M. (Polly) Hacking 16. Bill Taylor (hairdresser) 17. Miss C. M. Bellhouse (of Hope Anchor) 18. Walter Stocks 19. E. D. Compton 20. Harry Schofield (grocer) 21. Frederick Orford (postmaster) 22. George Cade 23. Ben Sharpe 24. Thomas Morse.

21 Cartoon by Philip Burne-Jones from his letter to E. F. Benson of September 11th 1910 . . . "no one to play golf-croquet with, and no croquet implements nor lawn whereon to play, if there were."

Index

Acton, Harold, 90
Adams, Joseph, 96–7
Addington, 13, 18
Aiken, Conrad, 64, 94
  Jane, 94
  Joan, 94
  Dr John, 64, 94
Aldington, Mrs, and Richard, 94
Alexandra, Queen, 68–9
Alice, Princess, Countess of Athlone, 38, 57–8, 62–3
Anchorites, 65, 94
Anderson, Mary, 14, 90
Anstruther, Admiral, 98
Arthritis, 20–1, 44, 54–5, 57–8, 61, 69, 88
Ashby, Elizabeth (*née* Ellis), 62, 92
Askwith, Lady, 69–70
  Betty, 69–70, 90
Athlones, 38, 57–8, 62–3
Austin, Alfred, 69
Avocet, 27

Bach, J. S., 13, 24, 29, 64
Batcheler family, 92
Bayley, Mrs Viola, 63
Beasley, John K., 93
Bell, Dr, 24
Bellhouse, Miss Constance, 94
Bendall, Captain Geoffrey, 50, 89, 94
Benge, Nurse, 95
Benson, A. C. (Arthur), 11, 12, 15, 19, 23, 27, 35, 36–7, 90, 97
  Edward Frederic, *passim*
  Edward White, 11–16 *passim*, 18, 26, 27, 28, 47, 71
  Maggie, 12, 14, 15–16, 26–7, 44, 46
  Martin, 12
  Mrs (Mary), 11–16 *passim*, 26–8, 32–5, 70, 71, 88
  Nellie, 14, 90
  R.H. (Hugh), 13, 16, 70–1
Best, William, 94
Birdwatching, 19, 27, 32, 37, 48
Bligh, 65–6
Bowen, Mr, 94, 96
Breads, John, 17
Broadway, in the Cotswolds, 84, 90
Brougham, Hon. Eleanor, 51, 56, 67
Brown, F. Yeats-, 35, 47, 49, 52, 56, 88, 89
Bryan, William, 64, 96
Burne-Jones, Philip, 46 (and see his cartoon)
Burnhams, 31, 32, 44, 50, 53
Burra family, 24, 89, 96. *See also* Ritchie, Lady
Bushby, John, 91
  Queenie, 91
Butterflies, 12, 13, 61
Button, Dr, 97

Cambridge, 14, 23, 27, 37, 47, 48, 67
Canterbury, Archbishops of. *See* Benson, Edward White; Davidson, Abp R.; Lang, Abp Cosmo; Tait, Abp A.
Capri, 16, 19, 28, 41, 90
Carey, William, 31–2
Carnell, Clara May, 70–1
Chess, 19, 40, 42, 64, 65, 95
Chilton family, 92
Christmas, 31, 50, 58, 60
Colefax, Lady Sybil, 70, 90
Cooper, Beth, 12
Corelli, Marie, 91
Cory, Captain, 96
  Rose d'Almeida, 96
Crawley, Nurse Kate, 91, 92
Crooke, Richard Lawless, 93
Crosskill, Mrs Betty (*née* Hacking), 65
Crown. *See* Dogs . . .

Daukes, Major and Mrs Archie, 47–8, 56
Davidson, Abp R., 27–8, 35
Dawes, Captain Edwin, 24, 56, 96
Deacon, Mr, 98
Deason, Albert, 93
Death and funeral of E. F. Benson, 23–4, 29, 55–6, 61–2, 66
Delves, Mr, 22, 63
Depression, E. F. Benson's, 16, 54–5
Desborough, Lord, 69
Dogs, collie, 12, 28, 46, 50, 52–3, 57, 59, 62
Donovan family, 92
Dowling, Misses, 24
Droitwich Spa, 53, 90

East Sheen, Temple Grove, 13, 25
Eaton, George, 24
Edward VIII, 46–7
Edwards, Rose. *See* Tomlin
Ellis, H. Snow, 91
Ellis, Humphrey, 39, 94

Ellis family, 62, 92, 93
Evacuees, 58

Fannon, John, 92
Farquharson, Mrs, 46, 51
Farrow. *See* Carnell
Fletcher, Percy, and family, 92
Fowler, Constance. *See* Warrender
  Canon John, 19, 24, 27, 49–50, 58, 59–62, 95
Franks, Miss, 49–50
  Mr, 95
Freedom of the Borough of Rye, E. F. Benson's, 23, 28, 66
Funeral of E. F. Benson. *See* Death . . .

Gabriel, 36
Garden Room, *passim*
George V, 47, 57
Ghosts and the supernatural, 14, 61, 64, 66, 68, 88
Gladstone, W. E., 14, 15
Godden, Rumer, 44
Golden Hind model, 23, 60–1
Golf, 19, 32, 38, 39, 40, 45, 47, 50, 53, 88, 94, 97
Gourlay, Nettie, 15
Greave, Mr, 94
Grebell, Allen, 17, 64, 68
Greece, 13, 14–15, 93
Green, Charlie, 94
  Ivy. *See* Robbins
Gurney, Miss, 40

Hacking, Betty. *See* Crosskill
  family, 96–7
  Polly, 65, 96–7

Hall, Radclyffe, 52, 58, 68, 87–8, 93, 97
Harratt, Dr, 97
Hichens, Tom, 89
Hogan, Mr, 28
Homosexuality, E. F. Benson's alleged, 24–7
Horsted Keynes. *See* Tremans
Hurst, Rev. John, 24

Irvine, Colonel, 98

Jacobs, A. R., 97
Jacomb-Hood, G. P., 93
  Mrs G. P., 21, 24, 50, 64, 67, 91, 93
James, Henry, 14, 18–19, 36, 44
  Henry, jr, 18, 54, 55
  William, 18, 44
Jenkins, J. Molyneux, 97

Kenwyn, Cornwall, 12
Kingdons, 96
King's Messenger, E. F. Benson as, 20, 37
Kingsland, Miss, 92

Lamb family, 16–18
Lamb House, Rye, *passim*. *See also* Secret Garden
Lambert, Mrs, 92
Lambeth Palace, 13, 35
Lang, Abp Cosmo, 28
Langdon, Eugenia, 27
Larpent, Miss de Hochepied, 24, 93
le Blond, Mrs Aubrey, 90
Lincoln, 12
Lister, Lady Evelyn, 55–6
Lister, Regie (Hon. Reginald), 15, 56
Lloyd, Mr, 88, 93
London, Brompton Square, *passim*
  Oakley Street, 15, 16, 35
Look-out (belvedere platform) given by E. F. Benson, 21, 83
Luck, Fanny, 92
Lutyens, 49
Luxmoore, H. E., 90

MBE, E. F. Benson awarded, 20, 37, 88
Macdonnell, J. H., 65–6, 94
McDowall family, 24, 52–3, 56
Magistrate, E. F. Benson as, 21, 62, 63, 66, 93
Mapp & Lucia books, *passim* and particularly in the Tilling Section at the end of the book
Marlborough College, 13–14, 25, 48
Marrot, 52
Marsden, George, 66, 92
Martin, Mrs, 93
Mary, Queen, 28, 47, 57
Mary Rose model, 23
Mason, Family, 92
  Mrs, 92–3, 96–7
Masters, Brian, 91
Mawle, Rose, 92
Mayor, E. F. Benson as, 21–2, 28, 55, 57, 66
Melba, Dame Nellie, 49, 59, 69, 89
Mickleson, Myfanwy, 57
Miles, Eustace, 14, 48, 88
  Philip and Sybil Napier, 93
Mimicry, 14, 49, 51
Moneypenny, Mrs K., 93
Monkhouse, Mrs, 96

Moreton, Captain and Mrs Claud, 94
Mylne, Major Boris, 71
Mrs Kathleen, 71
Mrs 'Tan', 71

Nichols, Beverley, 51–2, 89
Novello, Ivor, 51

Orford, Frederick, 97

Page, Mrs, 36
Piano, 13, 19, 35, 41, 44, 45, 58, 64, 88, 89, 90
Pigrome, Mr E. R., 24, 42, 64
Miss S. B. S., 64–5
Plank, George, 48–9, 55
Powell, James, & Sons, 28
Powles, Mrs, and Miss Veronica, 63–4, 89
Viola. *See* Bayley
Prentice, Geoffrey, 31

Ramsay, Miss D., 93
Ravenhill, Captain, 97
Recipes, by E. F. Benson, 22–3
Reeves, Major, 88, 97
Ann. *See* Hacking, Ann
Reid, Col. John Watt, 50, 88–9
Mrs, 50
Riseholme, Lincs., 12
origin of the fictitious, 84, 90, 91
Ritchie, Lady, 64
Robbins, Ivy, 24, 26, 29, 36, 53, 57–9, 92
Runciman, The Hon. Sir Steven, 7, 26, 64, 67–9, 90
Rye, *passim*. *See also* Secret Garden
Bonfire Boys, 31–2
Chess Club. *See* Chess
Club, 32
Conservative Club, 32
Golf Club. *See* Golf
Literary Institute/Society, 24, 42, 64–5
Museum, 40, 95
Parish Church, 24, 27–9, 50
Shops and businesses, *passim* and in particular, 97–8
Rylands, George, 19

Savernake Forest, 13, 61
Schofield, Harry, 98
Secret Garden, 21, 28, 61, 66, 80, 88
Severn, Arthur, 91
Shingles, 58, 88
Sidgwick, Mary. *See* Benson, Mrs (Mary)
Skating and Winter Sports, 13, 16, 39, 40, 44–5, 64
Skinner, Dr and Mrs, 62–3, 96
Margaret. *See* Wethey
Smith, Admiral Sir Aubrey Clare Hugh, 47, 65
Miss Josepha Aubrey, 65
Smyth, Dame Ethel, 52, 90
Spicer, 34, 35–6, 42
Sports, 13, 20–1, 27, 38, 39, 48. *See also* Golf, *and* Skating and Winter Sports
Stained glass windows. *See* Windows
Stanmore, Lord, 68
Stephen, Katharine, 74
Stocks, Walter, 98
Stonham, Edgar, 94
Stormonts, 96
Sturgis, Howard Oliver, 89
Supernatural, the. *See* Ghosts
Sussex Express, 24, 66
Swan, Percival, 94
Sykes, Mrs Harry, 92

Taffy. *See* Dogs . . .
Tait, A. (Abp), 14
Tait, Lucy, 14, 15, 34
Tayleur, Mr, 94
Taylor, Mrs, 33
Temple, Peter, 92
Tilling, 73–91
Tilling Society, 9, 69
Tomlin, Charlie and Rose, *passim* and in particular 31–56
Tremans, Horsted Keynes, 15, 19, 32–6 *passim*, 39, 44, 46
Troubridge, Una, Lady, 68, 88, 93, 97
Truro, 12, 46
Tupper, Lady, 94

Vidler, Dr Alec, 95
Leopold Amon, 40, 94–5
Vincent, Captain Dacre, 50, 96
Mrs Dacre, 91, 96

Wallis, H. H., 91, 97
Warrender, Mrs Constance (*née* Fowler), 24, 50, 58, 59–62, 88, 95–6
Lady Maud, 19, 24, 36, 59, 96
Wellington College, 11, 14
Wethey, Mrs Margaret (*née* Skinner), 62–3, 96
Williams, J. C., 24
Willingdon, Lord, 22, 28
Windows, stained glass, 21, 27–9
Winter sports. *See* Skating and

Woods, Aubrey, 75
Wyse, John, 69, 86

Yeats-Brown, F. *See* Brown